Problem situations
in teaching

PROBLEM SITUATIONS IN TEACHING

Gordon E. Greenwood
Thomas L. Good
Betty L. Siegel

UNIVERSITY
PRESS OF
AMERICA

LANHAM • NEW YORK • LONDON

Copyright © 1971 by
Harper & Row, Publishers, Inc.

University Press of America,™ Inc.

4720 Boston Way
Lanham, MD 20706

3 Henrietta Street
London WC2E 8LU England

Printed in the United States of America

Reprinted by arrangement with
Harper & Row, Publishers, Inc.

Library of Congress Cataloging in Publication Data

Greenwood, Gordon E., 1935-
    Problem situations in teaching.

    Reprint. Originally published: New York : Harper &
Row, 1971.
    Bibliography: p.
    1. Teaching—Addresses, essays, lectures.
2. Problem children—Education—Addresses—
essays, lectures. 3. Learning disabilities—Addresses,
essays, lectures. I. Good, Thomas L., 1943-
II. Siegel, Betty L., 1931-   . III. Title.
LB1027.G72   1983   371.1'02   83-5784
ISBN 0-8191-3089-3 (pbk.)

Contents

Preface

Too often the authors of this book, during their careers as public school teachers and as teachers of teachers, have heard graduates and undergraduates in teacher training say that some education course that they had just taken was a waste of time. The complaint most often heard goes something like this. "All that theory the prof expected me to memorize and parrot back to him on an exam has nothing to do with the real world of teaching." In psychological terms the student feels that the facts and principles to which he has been exposed have little transfer value.

There are many reasons why the theory presented in an education course lacks transfer value to the student. For one, it may not be presented in an organized and integrated way so that it "hangs together" for the student. In other words, sets of organized principles that the student can later apply to the teaching situation are not presented as such. In many classes instructors do provide their students with meaningfully organized sets of principles which can, potentially, be applied to later teaching situations. However, if these students do not learn these principles and the process for applying them, very little of their course knowledge is likely to transfer to actual teaching situations.

There are many factors which make it difficult for the college instructor to provide his students with application opportunities. It often isn't easy to get public schools, or for that matter even laboratory schools associated with colleges of education, to permit education students to try out the theories they are learning. Micro-teaching equipment, computer-assisted techniques, and even films are often too expensive for many colleges to obtain. As a result, the college instructor often settles for giving examples of application during his lecture.

This book is an attempt to provide material that can be used for application purposes in teacher education courses. The problem situations presented have been developed from real ones as described to the authors by teachers who faced them. Of course, the decisions that the teachers made in dealing with the problems have been deleted. Each situation presented in the book may therefore be said to be problem-centered in the sense that it is left open-ended and unresolved. Such problem situations provide opportunities for students in teacher education to develop their decision-making skills.

In the introductory chapter a process or strategy for making decisions about such problem situations is outlined. Both research and our experience indicate that education students who engage in problem-centered, decision-making activities learn to expect and to accept such problems as a normal part of a teacher's activities. The authors feel that the most profitable teacher attitude is the one that says, "I recognize that *I* have yet another problem. What can *I* realistically do to deal with it?"

It is the authors' experience that the problem situations presented in this book lend themselves to many different types of instructional activities. For example, the instructor can let his students attack the problems individually or in small groups while he serves as a guide and a resource person. Also, the open-ended aspect of the problems permits them to be utilized as stimuli for role-playing activities. If the instructor prefers more conventional procedures the problems are useful, especially with the assistance of the questions that follow each problem case, as stimuli to class discussion. We hope the instructor will feel free to adapt the use of these materials to best fit his unique course as he attempts to "teach for transfer."

One approach that the authors have found useful in educational psychology courses is to ask the students to eventually deal with such questions as the following during their decision-making activities. (1) What, in psychological terms, is the nature of the problem faced by the teacher? (2) Can you state the psychological theory or set of principles that you have applied? Is it backed by research? (3) Can you cite evidence from the case to support the application of each of the theories or principles that you have applied? (4) Can you suggest operational and feasible courses of action that the teacher can take to deal with the problem? Are they consistent with the theory that you have applied? Have you considered both long-range and immediate courses of action? (5) How could the teacher check to make sure that the courses of action you have suggested are working?

The authors are deeply indebted to Dr. David Gliessman, Dr. Laurence Brown, and Dr. Richard Turner of the Educational Psychology Department at Indiana University for many of the ideas that are contained in this book. While the material in this book is strictly the responsibility of the authors, Dr. Gliessman, Dr. Brown, and Dr. Turner greatly influenced the thinking of the senior author while he was a graduate student at Indiana University.

We wish to acknowledge the assistance given by the Institute for the Development of Human Resources, University of Florida, Ira J. Gordon, Director. Thanks are especially due to Peggy Scott, Roxie Peyton, Sue Kirkpatrick, Jan Larson, and Suzi Good for typing the manuscript. We offer a special thanks to Martha Weldon and Kay Ernst for their valuable assistance.

This book could not have been written without the contributions of the teachers who took the time to report to us the data surrounding the problem cases we have presented. We especially appreciate the efforts of Etoy Ashley, Bernadette Augustin, Alfreida Hudson, Frederick A. Jones, Nancy Nash, Ray D. Nelson, and Dale Underwood, the seven teachers who wrote both the problem situation and decision paper for "Joe Defies Authority," which is presented in the introduction.

Finally, the authors wish to thank their wives, husband, and children for their encouragement, understanding, and patience. It is to them that this book is dedicated.

Gordon E. Greenwood
Thomas L. Good
Betty L. Siegel

Problem situations
in teaching

The relationship between educational theory and teaching: a point of view

The teacher as decision-maker

Teaching is an extremely important but highly complex art. Many attempts have been made to determine and describe the nature of the art. S me educational scientists have attempted to evaluate teaching by distinguishing between good or effective teaching and bad or ineffective teaching (Biddle and Ellena, 1964).

It is our position that a wholly satisfactory description of the essence of good teaching has not yet been derived, although many promising developments have occurred in the last two decades, particularly in the branch of educational psychology called "teacher behavior." Behavioral scientists like Amidon and Hunter (1966), Medley and Mitzell (1963), Brown (1968), and Brophy and Good (1969) have developed instruments to systematically observe various aspects of the behavior of teachers and pupils in the classroom. If these instruments can be shown to relate to changes in such variables as pupil achievement, creativity, self-concept, etc., they would seem to hold great promise for identifying different aspects of good and bad teaching. Once these instruments have proven themselves by research, it might then be possible for the teacher to learn to classify his own behavior and change it.

At the present time systematic observation of teacher behavior is still in the early stages of its development. Much research has yet to be conducted and systematic observation instruments covering the many different aspects of teaching have yet to be constructed. However, even if it becomes possible to classify a teacher's behavior as effective or ineffective, the teacher will still have to decide what to do that might be effective in a problem situation. If a predetermination of teacher effectiveness cannot be achieved, teachers will, of course, continue to make decisions.

The authors of this book hold the following view of teacher behavior and teacher education.

1. Decision-making is a critical aspect of the teacher's job.
2. The teacher typically makes decisions on the basis of his personal belief system, which we prefer to call his theory.
3. Education courses should help the teacher examine and state his theory and give him the opportunity to integrate it with many scientific educational theories.
4. Education courses should permit the teacher to develop his decision-making skills by giving him the opportunity to make decisions on the basis of the theories that he is learning. (The authors have attempted to provide one type of decision-making opportunity in the form of the actual teaching problems that follow this section.)

THE ROLE OF EDUCATIONAL THEORIES IN DECISION-MAKING

The teacher is not likely to have a theory in the scientific sense of the word. That is, he is not likely to be able to state a carefully defined and consciously held set of generalizations that are systematically related to one another and inductively derived from and systematically tested by empirical research (Gordon, 1968). His theory might better be called a "system of beliefs" (Brown, 1968), or a "field of perceptions" (Combs and Snygg, 1959), or a "philosophical position" (Gordon, 1968). Our bias is to refer to the system of generalizations that actually governs the teacher's behavior as his theory. In this sense of the term, virtually all teachers have a theory. It is our belief that if teachers clarify and systematize their beliefs they will become more adept in interpreting classroom behavior and more capable of devising strategies.

Each teacher seems to have a personalized theory of education. For example, a teacher may operate from a consciously or unconsciously held set of generalizations like the following. "In order for the kids in my class to learn, they must keep busy and work hard. Other types of behavior are not conducive to learning and therefore are not desirable. I must keep good discipline by being firm and consistent in my disapproval and punishment of undesirable behavior. On the other hand, I must be fair and not favor certain kids as I reward those students who behave in desirable ways."

The above set of generalizations contains complex and interrelated psychological and philosophical assumptions. Upon examining the teacher's complete theory, we would find still other generalizations relating to curriculum, objectives, teaching methods, and so forth. It is a good bet that the generalizations held by the teacher mentioned above will be tested only by personal experience since he is not likely to examine the psychological theory and research implied in them, much less conduct research himself. Personal experience alone is not an adequate test since it lacks the careful sampling procedures and objectivity characteristic of scientific research. Also, as you read the above generalizations, you probably wished that the teacher had defined certain words for you, like "busy," "work hard," and "other types of behavior." In short, because his theory is unsystematically stated, the teacher would have a hard time communicating it to someone else, much less testing it by research. Further, when something he does works well for him, he may not even be able to identify what he did so that he can try it again in a similar situation. It is indeed a pity when a great artist cannot adequately describe his technique to others so that they can emulate him or test his assumptions (Jackson, 1968).

However, some teachers will say, "My theory may not be very scientific but at least it is mine, and I *feel* that it has served me well. Many problems, especially discipline problems, happen too rapidly and require too quick a response for me to analyze them in terms of some scientific theory before I decide what to do about them. In such cases you just have to react from your gut." This reasoning requires examination.

First, the assumption is made that the individual teacher's theory, given the same level of comprehensiveness and relevance, is somehow better than scientifically developed theories, such as some of those in the area of psychology. While we agree, for example, that some psychological principles may certainly have more relevance or be more comprehensive than others in helping a teacher deal with a given teaching problem, we fail to see how a set of vague and scientifically untested generalizations about the world and about teaching can be superior to an empirically derived and carefully stated scientific theory. Should the teacher rely on experience alone in making classroom decisions? Shouldn't he be willing at least to examine and try out scientific theories?

The second assumption is that the teacher can react from his gut (which has to mean his own theory unless he acts without thinking) faster than he can from a scientific theory. We agree that he can because he has learned to respond this way. Who's to say, however, that he couldn't act just as rapidly from a scientific theory that he has become thoroughly familiar with and has "made his own." For example, a teacher who has made B. F. Skinner's (1969) principles concerning operant conditioning his own by applying and using them might be able to respond in terms of that theory as quickly as he could in terms of the one that he formerly held. Further, he might not find it necessary to respond so often on a spur of the moment basis if he takes Skinnerian principles into consideration when he is doing his planning.

The fact is, the teacher will make a decision of some kind whether it is based on a scientific theory or not. Even if he decides to ignore the problem, he has chosen a course of action (or inaction, as the case may be). If decision-making is viewed as the process of choosing between two or more alternative courses of action, it becomes obvious that often the teacher takes a risk and gambles when he chooses course A instead of course B. The question is whether he should base his decision on his experience-based theory alone or on his theory combined with empirically tested scientific theory. Any way he goes, he is gambling. Which is the safest bet? When the teacher takes the wrong course of action, his pupils ultimately end up the losers.

TOWARD A SYSTEMATIC THEORY

How can prospective and experienced teachers begin to develop their theory of teaching and integrate it with scientific educational theory while taking teacher education courses? Perhaps a good approach for a teacher to take when he is taking a course in educational psychology (or, perhaps, for that matter, any course) would be for him to: (1) examine and state his own theory (or system of beliefs) under the direction of his instructor; (2) examine the various psychological theories, sets of principles, and concepts that seem to have relevance to teaching noting the strengths, weaknesses, and focuses of each; (3) determine which psychological theory or theories seem to be closest to his own; (4) compare and contrast the two, making any necessary revisions in his own theory while reserving the right to be an eclectic; (5) test the revised theory in the classroom. Testing can be done by the teacher engaging in his own "action research" as well as by reading about and participating in the research of others. In this way a teacher can retain his own theory, at least in revised form and likely in terms borrowed from "someone who is better at saying what I have always believed," and still be able to borrow from the strong points of several scientific theories.

In order for the teacher to begin to examine his personal theory he might try to answer as honestly and realistically as possible such questions as the following. (1) What causes students to behave the way they do? To what extent is student behavior a product of learning as opposed to heredity? (2) What is learning and what conditions are necessary for it to take place? (3) What is it necessary for the teacher to do to promote learning in the classroom? How can he tell when learning is taking place? (4) What is a discipline problem? At what point does a child become a discipline problem, and what techniques do you customarily use (or intend to use) to deal with such problems? (5) What can the teacher do to prevent such problems from arising or from happening again? (6) How can the teacher tell when he is doing his job effectively? (7) To what extent should the teacher be concerned with aspects of the student's growth other than academic achievement? On what aspect should primary emphasis be put?

A strategy for attacking teaching problems

Assuming that the teacher is faced almost daily with the task of making decisions about many different things, including, from time to time, difficult problems that he has not faced before; and further, assuming that the educational theory to which the teacher is exposed in his psychology, philosophy, methods, etc., courses is scientifically based and does have application value, why do many teachers not use such theory in their decision-making activities? Part of the answer may lie in the fact that teachers have not learned in their education courses how to use theory right along with learning the theory itself. That is, they have not learned and developed a process or strategy for making decisions about the kinds of problems that face them in their work.

Another reason may be that educational theory is not presented in an organized, integrated, and meaningful way. Some textbooks, for example in educational psychology, present a little motivation here, a little transfer of learning there, and a little self-concept somewhere else, so that it turns out to be a disconnected, disunited hodgepodge of facts and principles. Whole theories or meaningfully organized sets of principles that the teacher can examine to revise his own theory or to use as a frame of reference for making decisions about teaching problems are often not presented as such.

The purpose of this book is to provide typical teaching problems that the teacher can work through and thereby develop his own strategy for attacking such problems. It is assumed that he already has been exposed to educational theories or will learn them at the time he attacks a given problem. Perhaps he will even state and use his own theory. Be that as it may, how can a teacher arrive at a decision about a problem that confronts him?

First of all, there is probably no definite series of steps that each teacher should always attempt to follow in arriving at a decision. Steps that can be identified will not always follow one another in the same sequence. Each teacher will probably develop his own strategy. Furthermore, once a decision is made it also has to be executed and evaluated. The materials in this book are relatively limited in their capacity to provide the teacher with experiences in those important activities. Video-tape materials, such as those used in micro-teaching, would seem to be more suited to providing such experiences.

While referring the reader to more detailed accounts of the decision-making and problem-solving processes (such as those of McDonald, 1965; Dewey, 1910; Kilpatrick, 1936; Perkins, 1969), let us examine what the teacher goes through in arriving at a decision about a problem that confronts him. Remember, while the steps suggested here all seem quite essential, the sequence suggested is only one way in which the teacher can proceed.

1. RECOGNIZING A PROBLEM AND DECIDING TO DEAL WITH IT

The thing that the teacher must do first is recognize that a problem exists and decide to do something about it. As has been pointed out, some teachers are quite unaware that certain problems exist while others simply refuse to acknowledge their existence. Still others recognize the existence of a given problem but refuse, for one reason or another, to do anything about it.

In any case, the teacher is likely to recognize that a problem exists and decide to do something about it if some external or internal pressure convinces him that he should. External pressures like parents, principals, other teachers, and even students often cause certain teachers to face problems that they would just as soon avoid. The most obvious internal pressure that influences the teacher's behavior is his own theory. Whereas Teacher A may interpret a given student's behavior as quite desirable, Teacher B may interpret the same behavior as a serious problem and decide to do something about it. For example, the teacher who is primarily concerned with good discipline and pupil achievement may not interpret little Mary Smith's highly anxious, introverted, and socially withdrawn behavior as problem behavior. He may see it as quite desirable since Mary is a hard worker and never a discipline problem, even when the teacher leaves the room. (See Lindgren, 1967, p. 173.)

Of course, teaching is not all problems. Teachers make decisions about many things and, in the case of many of them, choose between two or more alternatives that are well known to them. For example, "Shall I teach the world history unit on ancient Greece the way that I taught it last semester or shall I teach it the way I taught it the semester before that?" In such cases the teacher may feel that it is not necessary to consider new and unfamiliar courses of action.

It is also true that even the best of teachers has days during which he is not faced with making any decisions at all. Certainly some routine or habitual responding by the teacher is not only desirable, but is often the only way that he can preserve his sanity. One often wonders, however, how much time a good teacher can spend in routine responding without engaging in any diagnostic, decision-making activity. Unless a teacher at least periodically examines or evaluates the effects of his routine responding, he probably won't remain a good teacher for very long. A decision that applies to one situation may very well not apply to another.

It should be pointed out that the teacher of today seems to have decided to deal with a broader range of problems than did the teacher of a few decades ago. The decision to go on strike for various reasons and to become active in politics are obvious examples. Some other recognized problems that lie outside the classroom but nevertheless affect it are such things as working with a hostile principal, handling interfering parents, and dealing with the problem teacher in the room next door. The point is, today's classroom teacher has decided to deal with problems other than those of individual pupils. At the same time, it is probably true that all of the problems that the teacher has decided to do something about eventually affect the classroom in one way or the other.

2. GATHERING DATA TO EXAMINE THE NATURE OF THE PROBLEM

Once the teacher recognizes that a problem exists and decides to deal with it, he must then fully and objectively examine the nature of the problem. Take the case of a teacher named Mrs. Jones who, as far as she is concerned, has two problems: Mary and Johnny. Mary is constantly seeking attention and disrupting class while Johnny is bored and goes to sleep. What can she do about them? In the first place, she probably needs to gather more information before she does anything. Part of the problem may be with Mrs. Jones. Has she attempted to find out what interests Johnny and the rest of her students? Is her classroom a stimulating place that is full of interesting activities? Does she positively reinforce what she considers to be desirable behavior on Mary's part? Does she assume that Mary is just like another girl that she had a few years ago and that she should treat her the same way that she did the other child? To decide to deal with the problem and, to take the second step, to examine fully in an objective way the nature of the problem, could indeed prove to be a very threatening experience for Mrs. Jones.

One of the first things that the teacher will do in examining the nature of the problem is to gather data. It is important to note that the kind of data that the teacher will gather will be limited by the theory from which he operates. For example, one teacher might systematically examine the cumulative record of every one of his students. Another teacher might make a point of never looking at cumulative records because he believes that they might bias him. (If the latter sounds ridiculous, see Rosenthal and Jacobson, 1968.)

What kind of data can the teacher gather? The answer, of course, is that it all depends upon the type of problem he is dealing with and whatever limitations his theory places upon him. Perhaps the teacher might begin by asking himself what has occurred to cause him to decide that a problem exists. More often than not it will be something that somebody said or did: in other words, what the psychologist calls behavior. What a student says or does, something that another teacher says or writes in a cumulative record, things observed in a student's home during a visit, a student's performance on an essay exam, a student's score on an intelligence test, the comments of a student or parent during a conference or informal conversation, student interests, ambitions, and hobbies stated in autobiographical compositions or pictured in drawings, and many other things are all data that may or may not be of use to the teacher (Perkins, 1969, 25–39).

One of the most difficult things for a teacher to learn to do is to be objective about his data-gathering. For one thing, he must learn to distinguish between actual behavioral events and inferences and generalizations that he makes about such events. Also, he must examine himself and realize that as a human being he has certain biases, values, attitudes, and ego defenses which may interfere with his objectivity. He must learn to be both witness and lawyer when examining data that he has gathered. Like a good attorney he must learn to cross-examine himself and ask, "Is that what Johnny actually said or did I just infer that he was talking about me?"

To illustrate this point, consider Mr. Smith, who has frequently observed two students in his senior civics class, Jean and Shirley, whispering together in the back of the room. He has always ignored this behavior, hoping that it would disappear. The two girls are very physically attractive to Mr. Smith and very popular among their classmates. He wanted to befriend them, but they seemed to make fun of him at times. Once when he tripped over a wastebasket, they seemed to laugh louder and longer at him than anyone else in the room. At other times, they would whisper together, look in his direction, and begin to giggle.

Mr. Smith was not very popular when he was a student in high school. He was shy around girls, dated very little, and did not participate in varsity athletics although he wanted to be admired and popular. He wanted to be a doctor but became a teacher, primarily because he felt that the local teachers college was the only place he could afford to attend, and he was reasonably sure he could do the academic work required of him.

On the day in question, another teacher had hurt his feelings by criticizing the tie he had worn to school. The other teacher had said, "Man, you're never going to be a swinger as long as you wear square ties like that." During second-period civics class, Jean and Shirley once again whispered together in the back of the room, looked in Mr. Smith's direction, and began to laugh. Mr. Smith inferred from their behavior that they were talking about him. He told them to go to the Dean of Girls' office.

The Dean of Girls later told Mr. Smith that the girls had been telling one another jokes. Mr. Smith didn't really believe this story and told the girls in no uncertain terms that he was going to move them away from each other and that the next time they talked he would cut their grades. Both girls had confused and bewildered expressions on their faces and Jean began to cry. Shirley said, "Why are you treating us this way, Mr. Smith? We always thought that you were the one teacher we have who really understands us!"

You can probably think of a great number of things that you would like to find out about Jean, Shirley, Mr. Smith, and others before you begin to diagnose this case. A good starting point is to consider Mr. Smith's objectivity. Was he objective in examining the data? From a measurement standpoint objectivity of this kind refers to the amount of agreement between observers. If two other teachers had observed the same behavior as Mr. Smith observed, would they have made the same inferences from the behavior of Jean and Shirley?

If Mr. Smith could remove his perceptual blinders for a moment what would he have actually observed about Jean and Shirley's behavior, and what would he have inferred? He has definitely seen the two girls whispering together, glancing at him, and laughing from time to time. He could probably even guess how many times they have engaged in this behavior if it were important. He did hear and see them laugh loud and long when he tripped over the wastebasket. Furthermore, the Dean of Girls said that the girls said they were telling jokes on the day that he sent them out of class. Finally, we know exactly what the girls said to Mr. Smith when he talked to them later because we have an exact quote. We can't see the girls' faces or hear the way in which Shirley said what she did to Mr. Smith. Our data have many limitations, but do provide some clues and suggest the need to collect additional information.

What kinds of inferences did Mr. Smith make from the behavioral data and are there other interpretations that could be made? First, he seemed to feel that the girls saw him as an inadequate male. Second, he inferred that they were whispering and giggling about him and his inadequacies. After the reported incident, he said that he refused to accept Shirley's statement concerning his adequacy as an understanding teacher. Are other inferences concerning the girls' behavior possible? Did Mr. Smith respond to the behavior that he observed or did he respond to the inferences that he drew from the behavior?

Imagine Mr. Smith and some other teachers at some future point in time in the teachers' lounge during their planning period. Imagine another teacher saying, "I have Jean Sinders and Shirley Merrick in my class this semester. Boy, what lookers! Hey, George, didn't you have some trouble with them last semester?" Mr. Smith says, "I sure did! They were always disrupting the class. Every time I turned my back they were whispering and giggling and making all kinds of noise."

Of course, no one in the lounge will ask George to state the behavioral evidence on which he is basing the above generalizations, but the important thing to recognize is that they are generalizations. How accurate are they? What sort of expectations will they create in the mind of the teacher who asked George about the two girls? To summarize, behavioral events are not the same thing as inferences and generalizations.

3. INTERPRETING THE DATA

The second thing that the teacher must do to determine the nature of the problem is to interpret the data in terms of a theory (whether personal or scientific). As has already been said, the teacher's theory (set of beliefs, perceptions, etc.) limits the kind of data that he gathers in the first place. At the same time, it may suggest other kinds of data that the teacher should attempt to gather. From the standpoint of perceptual psychology (see Rogers, 1951), for example, Mr. Smith should probably have attempted to have some sort of a conference with the girls to find out how they perceive him and the classroom situation.

When a teacher interprets the data in terms of a theory or theories or a set of principles, he is obviously making inferences and reaching generalizations in terms of the theory. It is at this point that the principles and concepts contained in textbooks, lectures, and discussions in theory courses can become relevant. Needless to say, the more scientific (in the sense of being supported by empirical research) such principles are, the greater their potential would seem to be.

4. ARRIVING AT A DECISION

Finally, after interpreting the data in terms of his theory, the teacher decides either to gather more data, to take a certain course of action that follows from or is consistent with the way in which he interprets the situation, or to do nothing at present (perhaps hoping that the problem will take care of itself). Of course, when the teacher operates from his own gut level or personal-experience-based theory, the whole process from recognition of the problem to decision may take only an instant. The more systematic the teacher tries to be, the longer it is likely to take, especially at first. Gathering and examining data objectively and interpreting them in terms of a carefully stated and tested theory are not skills that one learns quickly.

CONSISTENCY BETWEEN THEORY AND DECISION

No matter how long it takes to choose a course of action after interpreting a situation, the decision reached should be consistent with the theory used in interpreting the problem—that is, if the theory used is the real one that the teacher operates from. A gap seems to exist between theory and practice when a teacher self-reports that he operates from one set of beliefs but really operates from another (Brown, 1968).

When operating from a scientific theory that he has not yet fully made his own, he has a problem with making his decision consistent with the interpretation. Consistency is possible only to the extent that the teacher fully understands the theory. For example, understanding that Bobby has a high IQ but doesn't believe that he can succeed in his schoolwork, even if one knows something about the self-concept, doesn't necessarily suggest what the teacher ought to do about the situation unless he has considered the educational implications of perceptual psychology. The point is, however, that if the theory used has application value and the teacher has examined its application value, then it should suggest courses of action for him to follow in dealing with the problem. One way, then, to evaluate courses of action chosen by a teacher is to examine their consistency or the extent to which they logically follow from the theory utilized. This, in turn, leads back to an examination of the soundness and educational implications of the theory used to interpret the problem in the first place.

FEASIBILITY AND OPERATIONALITY OF THE DECISION

The course of action that the teacher has decided to follow should meet at least two other criteria: feasibility and operationality. Feasibility means that the course of action is something that the teacher can reasonably expect to do within the limits of the situation in which he finds himself. If the teacher decides to do such things as change school board opinion, or give all of his students a Stanford-Binet, or work with many of his students individually after school, he had better take into consideration the skills, the time and money, and the amount of effort and dedication that such endeavors require.

Operationality means that once the teacher has interpreted the problem in terms of a scientific theory, for example, and decided in theoretical terms what he should do about it, he must translate his theoretical decision into the actual operations that he intends to perform or get others to do. Such theoretical decisions as "helping George see himself in more positive ways," and "using praise and approval as reinforcers to encourage Mary to work harder," must be translated into actual classroom operations. Is the teacher going to use client-centered counseling techniques (see Rogers, 1951) with George in one-to-one counseling sessions after school? Is Mary's teacher going to verbally praise her each time she recites in class or sits still and studies for five minutes?

From such examples it should be obvious that feasibility and operationality often interact with one another. If something isn't stated operationally (for example, "What the teacher should do is try to meet each child's individual needs") it is often hard to tell whether it is feasible or not. However, the difference between the two can be seen clearly in ridiculous recommendations: "What the teacher should do is walk right up to the student, grab his belt with the left hand and his leg with the right, carry him to the nearest window, and throw him out." Although the course of action intended is stated in fairly operational terms, it is unfeasible.

Once a feasible and operational decision has been reached, the teacher must then execute and evaluate it. One of the variables that he is likely to have to evaluate is the effect of his own behavior on others. Systematic observation should prove a valuable tool for this purpose. If the decision turns out to be a poor one, the teacher should try to determine what went wrong. Even this procedure will be influenced by the theory he uses when he evaluates his decision. If a teacher is rigid and dogmatic, he is not likely to consider changing his theory in the face of unexpected results. He will probably deny that the results are bad or defend his theory in some way. One of the most effective ways for a teacher to defend his theory is to deny that he has one and to be suspicious of all theories, including scientific ones.

The discussion above suggests certain criteria that a teacher could use in evaluating his decision after he decides how to deal with a problem. He should ask himself the following questions. (1) How clearly defined and stated is the theory that I am applying to this problem and how does it square with scientific research? (2) How objective and thorough have I been in gathering and examining data? (3) Does the theory fit this problem in the sense that it fully explains and, in turn, is supported by the data I have gathered? (4) Is my decision consistent with my interpretation of the problem in terms of the theory that I have used? (5) Is my decision *feasible* and *operational* in its present form? The reader should apply these criteria to the decision reached in the problem situation that follows.

Joe defies authority

The problem situation, "Joe Defies Authority," was written by seven teachers in a graduate educational psychology course entitled Psychology in Teaching taught by one of the authors of this book. The problem was one which a member of the group actually had faced as a teacher. He therefore served as the primary source of data for the group. Both the problem situation and the analysis and decision that follow it are reproduced here in the form in which they were turned in to the instructor of the course after the group had worked on it for approximately eight class hours. Only minor changes have been made to make it fit more easily into this part of the book. Neither the problem nor the decision reached by the group is the best or the worst that the authors have seen in terms of the criteria discussed. They were chosen primarily because the written performance is typical and because the type of problem dealt with is of interest to most teachers.

SETTING: A small, relatively new high school in a rural area of a southeastern state.

TIME: Lunch period on a warm autumn day.

Mr. Nash, on hall duty, is standing in the doorway, because students are not permitted in the building at this time.

Joe, a large, muscular 19-year-old senior, whom Mr. Nash recognizes as one of his students in American history, approaches the door. Mr. Nash had been warned that Joe was a troublemaker, but had experienced no trouble with him himself.

Mr. Nash: You can't come in the hall now. You know students aren't allowed in here at this time.

Joe: (Stalling belligerently) I want some water.

Mr. Nash: You have to wait until the bell sounds.

Joe, ignoring Mr. Nash, walks to the water fountain and gets a drink.

Mr. Nash: I told you you couldn't get water.

Joe: (Insolently) I've already gotten it now.

Mr. Nash says nothing more and Joe walks outside. Shortly after this incident, Mr. Nash goes to the principal to secure information about Joe. From the disciplinary file, Mr. Nash learns that Joe has been a problem child through the years. He learns that Joe at one time had threatened a teacher with a knife, and has a reputation for tormenting other children, and shows no respect for authority. The file indicates that Joe had been reprimanded both physically and verbally. Scholastically, he appears to be average.

Joe lives with his grandmother. He never knew his father and was abandoned by his mother when he was eight months old. His grandmother is unable to discipline him, but she is concerned and cooperates with the school.

A few days later while Mr. Nash is conducting American history class, Joe loiters in the hall after the last bell rings. He then comes into class late expecting to be sent out as is the school policy for tardiness, but he is ignored by Mr. Nash.

Joe takes his assigned seat in the back of the classroom and pulls out a comic book instead of entering into the discussion. He keeps glancing at Mr. Nash as though daring him to say something, but Mr. Nash calmly ignores him and teaches the class.

At the end of the class period Mr. Nash calls for the papers that had been assigned. All the students but Joe hand them in. Mr. Nash says nothing as Joe walks by without handing in his paper.

The next day Joe is on time for class. He takes Brenda's seat.

Brenda: Get out of my seat, Joe.

Joe looks at her daringly, Brenda goes to Mr. Nash in the front of the room.

Brenda: Joe's in my seat.
Mr. Nash: Joe, you know where your seat is. Will you please sit where you belong.
Joe: I'll sit where I want to.
Mr. Nash: You'll sit where you are supposed to sit or we'll go to see the principal.

Joe grudgingly goes to his seat. An hour later, the class is dismissed.

Mr. Nash: Joe, will you remain after class for a few minutes?

Joe hesitates, then comes grudgingly.

Mr. Nash: Joe, what happened to your assignment that was due yesterday?
Joe: I didn't get around to doing it. I'll turn it in later.
Mr. Nash: See that you do. Why did you sit in Brenda's seat? I thought you and Brenda got along fairly well.
Joe: I was having a little fun with her, that's all.

Mr. Nash dismisses him.

A week later, Mr. Nash is in charge of admitting the students to the football game. Joe walks in without paying, and Mr. Nash follows him.

Mr. Nash: Don't you know you are supposed to pay?
Joe: So what?
Mr. Nash: Without a ticket, I can't admit you.

Joe ignores Mr. Nash and bolts into the stadium. The incident is reported to the principal and Joe is escorted from the game.

Joe's grandmother is interviewed by the principal the next day. She describes Joe as a problem at home also.

Grandmother: I have always tried to keep him in line. I used to use the strap on him several times a day, but now he's too big to whip. I guess he'll always be a bad boy. I've always said he'd be just like his no-good father.

The next day in the lounge during the teachers' break, several teachers are discussing Joe's conduct.

Mr. Nash: I'm concerned about Joe. I think he has a serious problem and we should do something to help him.

Mr. Evans (the shop teacher): I haven't had too much trouble with Joe in my class. In fact, Joe's one of my better students.

Mr. King (the math teacher): He's always late for my class and I won't let him in. You're just wasting your time on Joe.

Other teachers agree that it is a waste of time to work with Joe.

Later Mr. Nash meets Joe in the hall after school.

Mr. Nash: Come into the room, young man. I'd like to talk to you.

Joe: What's the matter? I didn't do anything wrong. You teachers are always picking on me.

Mr. Nash: I respect you, Joe. You are capable of doing fine work. What seems to be the problem? Have I done anything to offend you?

Joe: No.

Mr. Nash: Don't you think I respect you?

Joe: (Shrugs) I don't know.

Mr. Nash: What seems to be the problem then?

Joe: I don't have a problem. Nobody's gonna tell me what to do.

Mr. Nash: If you're to remain a part of this school community, you must obey the rules, just like everyone else.

Joe: I'm not like everyone else. You just don't want me around, that's all. Nobody does.

JOE DEFIES AUTHORITY: ANALYSIS AND DECISION

In the problem Joe is presented as a young man who lacks a sense of belonging ("You just don't want me around, that's all. Nobody does"). He defies rules and the people representing the enforcing authority for such rules ("Nobdy's gonna tell me what to do"). He uses his misbehavior as a plea for recognition from these same representatives of authority. The teacher "should realize that children misbehave not to annoy him but because they do not know of better ways of satisfying their needs; they are simply calling for help. . . . This is especially true of children with an unhappy home background who have to depend that much more on the teacher's understanding and acceptance."[1] Joe, having been left to the care of his grandmother, abandoned by his mother and father, certainly has not had a very happy or satisfying home life. The grandmother's statement

---

[1] G. J. Mouly, *Psychology for Effective Teaching,* 2nd ed. (New York: Holt, Rinehart & Winston, 1968), pp. 74–75.

to the principal ("I've always said he'd be just like his no-good father") indicates that Joe's childhood was filled with insecurity and the lack of affectionate relationships.

In Maslow's Hierarchical Theory of Motivation love and belonging are listed as basic needs.[2] Maslow developed a hierarchical order of needs required for a healthy, normal, and fully satisfying life. The five categories of needs are listed here:

1. Body needs—basic tissue needs—food
2. Safety needs—protection from harm or injury
3. Needs for love and belonging—warmth, status, acceptance, approval
4. Needs for adequacy, security, self-esteem, self-enhancement, competency
5. Needs for self-fulfillment, broader understanding

Maslow assumes that the physiological needs and safety needs are almost universally met due to the nature of our society. However, if one of these needs was not fulfilled, a person would be dominated with the obsession to satisfy that particular need; for example, hunger or thirst. If a man were thirsty, he would place his need for drink above all other needs. If the physiological needs were satisfied, the individual would then place in priority an unsatisfied need of the next higher order—safety or security.

Continuing along the hierarchy, we come to the belonging and love needs. If the lower two levels are satisfied, these needs emerge, causing the individual to seek friends and affectionate relationships.

The fourth order contains esteem needs:

These include the desire for a firmly based, high evaluation of the self. There is, in all of us, a desire for strength, for mastery and competence leading to a feeling of independence and freedom. In addition, individuals in our society seek prestige, dominance, and recognition from others. Satisfaction of the esteem needs generates feelings of worth, self-confidence, and adequacy. Lack of satisfaction of these needs results in discouragement, feelings of inferiority, and inadequacy.[3]

If the previous four needs are fulfilled, then the individual can satisfy the need for self-actualization. As Maslow says, "A musician must make music, an artist must paint, a poet must write, if he is ultimately to be at peace with himself. What a man *can* be, he *must be*. This need we may call self-actualization."[4] Maslow states that most of us are seeking the fulfillment of the lower-order needs. Not many of us are able to reach this self-actualizing stage. "It follows from this arrangement that, whereas the physiological needs may be met nearly one hundred per cent, each suc-

---

[2]J. P. Chaplin and T. S. Krawiec, *Systems and Theories of Psychology* (New York: Holt, Rinehart & Winston, 1960), p. 346.
[3]*Ibid.*, p. 348.
[4]A. H. Maslow, *Motivation and Personality* (New York: Harper & Row, 1954), p. 91.

cessive level will be satisfied to a lesser degree and the last on the list, the need for self-actualization, may go relatively unsatisfied."[5]

Relating Joe's school behavior to the first of Maslow's hierarchy of needs—that of the physiological nature—we see no evidence in Joe's appearance or in his actions of a deficiency. Neither does there seem to be a lack of the second order of safety needs. There is, however, evidence that Joe is in need of love and a sense of belonging ("You just don't want me around. Nobody does"). Joe never knew his father and was abandoned by his mother as a baby. The only home he has known is that provided by his grandmother. She seems to be annoyed by his presence and expresses openly her low opinion of him ("I guess he'll always be a bad boy. I've always said he'd be just like his no-good father").

Bakwin has noted that when children are separated from their mothers between the ages of six to nine months, the children develop a distrust of the world.[6] Joe shows this distrust of authority when he says: "What's the matter? I didn't do anything wrong. You teachers are always picking on me." Children establish an attitude toward authority during their first five years of living. The grandmother has been Joe's only symbol of authority at home ("I have always tried to keep him in line. I used to use the strap on him several times a day, but now he's too big to whip"). Because of her method of approaching Joe, it is no great surprise to see that he has formed a negative attitude toward authority. "Some [parents] reject their children openly and brutally, even to the point of abandoning them. . . . These children build up hate and hostility which they vent through retaliation against people and their property."[7] According to Mouly, "the rejecting home promotes . . . non-compliance."[8] Joe has definitely shown this non-compliance with his defiant disregard of the rules established by the school. Such defiance is demonstrated by Joe's actions in three incidents.

1. **Mr. Nash:** I told you you couldn't get water.
   Joe: (Insolently) I've already gotten it now.
2. **Mr. Nash:** Joe, you know where your seat is. Will you please sit where you belong.
   Joe: I'll sit where I want to.
3. **Mr. Nash:** Don't you know you are supposed to pay?
   Joe: So what?

The fourth and fifth needs, those of self-esteem and self-actualization, receive less attention since Joe is lacking in the third need for love and belonging. Maslow states that an individual concentrates all efforts on the

[5]Mouly, *op. cit.*, p. 73.
[6]Mouly, *op. cit.*, p. 97.
[7]Mouly, *op. cit.*, p. 494.
[8]Mouly, *op. cit.*, p. 495.

satisfaction of a need placed in priority over all the other needs.[9] Until Joe's needs for love and belonging are satisfied, he will continue to seek the satisfaction of these needs in undesirable ways, such as his defiance of authority.[10]

Jersild summarizes Joe's type of behavior in this way:

When parents are unreasonable or anxious, it can readily be seen that the growing child might begin to harbor the kind of quiet and chronic anger found in persons who feel abused, unfairly treated, or at least feel that they are treated with less consideration and respect than they deserve. If now, the child also is punished, and can never effectively fight back and "get even," feels discriminated against, feels that his parent or some other parent figure who stands over him not only is unreasonable and mean but actually dislikes him and is actively against him, then a strong grievance is in way of becoming established, and the child may have the beginnings of a deep grudge, a feeling that he would like to take revenge (even though he is helpless to do so). If this attitude becomes really acute, and nothing is done to ameliorate it, the child may develop an unresolved attitude of hostility. . . . In later childhood and adult life evidences of resistance and even active antagonism to authority figures often appear.[11]

To effectively resolve Joe's constant misbehavior at school and provide the relationship necessary for the satisfaction of Joe's need for love and belonging, Mr. Nash should follow three general courses of action.

1. He should develop and display a warm and accepting manner toward Joe.

A warm, accepting attitude is especially important for pupils who have already come to think of the world as hostile, critical, and exacting. And there are many children who acquire this unfortunate attitude early in life and who come to school with all the apprehension, fearfulness, and even defiance which such an attitude engenders. For this child who has had to accept more criticism than he can absorb, or who has had to face standards which he does not know how to meet, the teacher should be especially generous in his acceptance.[12]

Assuming that Mr. Nash is emotionally secure, he will then be able to give Joe this acceptance.

Specifically this basic acceptance or liking may be shown by the frequent and ungrudging use of praise. This need not be expressed in the form of a fulsome speech or in a sugary manner. A frequent enthusiastic exclamation, interjected sincerely and under conditions that are reasonably appropriate, would seem more natural and more effective. . . . Older pupils may suspect the sincerity of praise that bubbles continuously. Here the most

---

[9]Chaplin and Krawiec, op. cit., p. 346.

[10]Mouly, op. cit., p. 495.

[11]A. T. Jersild, Child Psychology, 4th ed. (Englewood Cliffs, N.J.: Prentice-Hall, 1954), pp. 383–384.

[12]J. M. Stephens, The Psychology of Classroom Learning (New York: Holt, Rinehart & Winston, 1965), p. 380.

useful test would probably be that of sincerity. If you do feel an admiration for the student's performance, give free vent to your feeling. . . .

Praise, certainly solemn praise, is not the only means of providing an atmosphere of acceptance. Many teachers can be hearty, jovial, or even rough, and yet give the child a feeling of acceptance and belonging.[13]

Also, in the water incident, Joe approaches Mr. Nash intent on defying the teacher's authority. Mr. Nash denies Joe permission to enter the hall, but he does not give Joe any reason for denying him a drink other than that it is a school rule ("You know you can't come in the hall now. You know students aren't allowed in here at this time"). Perhaps Mr. Nash can display a more warm and accepting manner with a comment such as: "Hi, Joe, I'm afraid I can't allow you in the building now. I'm sure you will understand what chaos we would have if everyone was in here running around. You see, most of the other teachers are at lunch now. I'll bet you can wait until the bell rings. If you collapse, I'll bring you a drink, okay?"

2. He should offer opportunities for accepting responsibilities within the school situations (showing confidence in Joe). Mr. Nash should give Joe daily responsibility in the room to make him feel closer and more "special" to his teacher. Possibly Joe could take attendance and see that every student is in his seat. (As a by-product of this action, Joe would also make it to class on time, and see the reasons for the punctuality rule. He would be receiving attention and gaining a feeling of belonging by helping Mr. Nash. Instead of opposing certain rules to gain attention, he could help uphold them. Gradually, as time allowed, Mr. Nash could place more emphasis on giving Joe certain responsibilities that required an amount of trust and affection on both Joe and Mr. Nash's part, such as running Mr. Nash's errands. After Joe fulfilled these duties, he could see Mr. Nash as a *person* in a role of authority not just an authority. This association could eventually transfer to other people in authority positions.[14]

3. Mr. Nash should improve Joe's social relationships with his peers by group interaction. This kind of group relationship could help Joe by substituting love and a sense of belonging which is lacking from his home environment.[15] Mr. Nash could give Joe a position of leadership and peer recognition by allowing Joe to moderate a panel concerned with current events. Or, he could allow Joe to supervise the construction of a project concerned with his area of study at the appropriate time.

To give Joe further experiences and opportunity for developing a sense of belonging, Mr. Nash should contact the shop teacher, Mr. Evans. Mr. Evans pointed out that he had experienced little trouble with Joe, and in fact, Joe was one of his better students. Perhaps the two teachers could design

[13]Stephens, *op. cit.,* p. 379.
[14]Mouly, *op. cit.,* p. 494.
[15]Stephens, *op. cit.,* p. 378.

a history project to be constructed in shop class. Such individual concern by both teachers would give Joe two situations in which to develop this sense of belonging and trust of authority.

If Mr. Nash wanted to gain further knowledge of Joe's problem, he could seek references such as the following:

Stephens, J. M. *Psychology of Classroom Learning,* 1965.
Mouly, G. J. *Psychology for Effective Teaching,* 1968.
Chaplin, J. P., and Krawiec, T. S. *Systems and Theories of Psychology,* 1960.
Cronbach, L. J. *Educational Psychology,* 1963.
Jersild, A. T. *Child Psychology,* 1954.
Maslow, A. H. *Motivation and Personality,* 1954.

After Mr. Nash initiated a warm and accepting manner, offered opportunities for responsibility, and improved Joe's social relationships, we would expect that Joe's attitude toward authority would improve. Joe should find socially acceptable methods for meeting his needs.

REACTIONS TO THE STUDENT PAPER

After examining the data that the group of seven teachers was able to put together and the decision that they reached, a student is likely to ask, "Well, is that the right answer?" Whether the decision reached is the right one or not depends, in the last analysis, on what happens when it is executed. The group that reached the decision would have to answer this question: "How could the teacher check to make sure that the courses of action you have suggested are working?" When this question has been answered then it becomes possible to evaluate the effects of the decision reached when it is executed.

However, even without testing the consequences of the decision reached it is still possible to examine the decision in terms of the criteria that we have suggested: "How clearly defined and stated is the theory that I am applying to this problem and how does it square with scientific research?" The theory used in this case is primarily Maslow's motivational or needs theory along with some principles concerning adolescent development and rebellion against authority that the teachers attempted to tie in with it.

How well do the teachers seem to understand Maslow and the other psychological principles? While the theory isn't systematically stated in depth and tied in with the psychological principles concerning rebellion, the teachers do seem to have at least a fair grasp of the essentials. They do not seem to have examined very extensively the research support for the theory and principles that they used. Most educational psychologists would probably agree that they need to dig deeper into their understanding of

Maslow and that they should examine the research support for that theory as well as for the other psychological principles that they mention.

What about the second question: "How objective and thorough have I been in gathering and examining data?" Again, the teachers do a fairly good job (for example, where they are able to actually quote what was said). However, some data are lacking in objectivity (for example, the data relating to the home life and the cumulative record), and further data could have been gathered. However, it should be taken into consideration that the teachers were looking back on a problem situation and could not reconstruct or obtain as much data as they would like to have.

The third question is: "Does the theory that I am using fit this problem in the sense that it fully explains and, in turn, is supported by the data that I have gathered?" While the teachers do attempt to cite behavioral evidence to support many of their contentions, the relationships existing between some of the psychological principles aren't always obvious (for example, between defiance on Joe's part and his need for love and belonging). But they do attempt to support their contentions and to explain the data they have assembled fairly well.

Let's move to the decision and combine and restate the fourth and fifth questions: Is the decision reached consistent with the theory used and is it feasible and operational? If one examines the courses of action suggested one by one, including the teachers' attempts to operationalize them, again we see that they do a fairly good job. Each course of action seems to follow from the psychological principles applied.

Feasibility and operationality suffer somewhat when one wonders about such things as how (operationality) Mr. Nash is going to arrange things so that he can bestow sincere warmth, acceptance, and praise upon Joe and bring about peer approval (feasibility). Consistency also suffers a bit in these two ideas since no attempt seems to be made to determine whether these activities would be need-reducing to Joe. The proposal that Mr. Nash contact Mr. Evans, the shop teacher, and work out a history project to be constructed in shop class would seem to be consistent with the theory used since shop seems to be need-reducing for Joe. This would be especially true if Mr. Nash would try to determine from Joe and Mr. Evans just why shop meets Joe's needs. Such a project should certainly provide Mr. Nash with an opportunity to praise Joe warmly and sincerely for his efforts. On the basis of available evidence, it would be a more consistent move to make Joe chairman of a construction of history projects committee than to make him moderator of a current events panel.

Of course, a panel of educational psychologists could severely pick apart the teachers' ideas in terms of the criteria suggested. Some would suggest that the problem could be better interpreted in terms of other psychological principles. However, the paper shows insight into the use of some psychological principles and these teachers are well on their way to making Maslow's theory their own.

A final note

Having presented a strategy for reaching decisions about teaching problems, the remainder of this book contains problem situations which teachers have actually faced and which can be used as you begin to develop or sharpen your own decision-making skills. First, a word about how the problem situations were developed.

The 20 problem situations presented in this book were selected from approximately 330 such problems obtained from over 100 teachers in at least 4 different states and representing a wide range of teaching experience. After initial descriptions of the problems were obtained, the problems were ranked by type. The authors then selected the problem situation they felt best represented each of the most often mentioned types of problems.

In writing each problem the authors have attempted to preserve as much of the original data as possible. When available the actual words spoken by the people involved are used. All names of people, schools, and places have, of course, been changed. Finally, an attempt was made to divide the problems as equally as possible between elementary, middle, and secondary school levels.

After most of the problem situations you will find data that may be of use to you, such as a page from a child's cumulative record, or a page from the teacher's grade book. You will then find a series of questions that may stimulate your thinking about the problem. These questions are primarily psychologically based and may not all be of equal value. Other questions (such as those relating to educational philosophy, curriculum, and teaching methods) could be raised just as validly as the ones that have been included.

Since the authors of this book are educational psychologists, we have naturally referred more to the psychological bases on which the other generalizations in a given theory tend to rest. It is no accident that educational psychology and educational philosophy are often referred to as "foundations courses" in colleges of education. This is because the concepts, principles, theories, and research studied in these courses underlie those studied in other education courses. While this chapter has concentrated more on the psychological bases of educational theory, it does not mean that educational theory outside the area of educational psychology is not important. Education professors would do well to remember that an individual teacher's theory is an integrated set of generalizations that cut across the lines of the various disciplines that are taught in a college of education; a teacher's theory is interdisciplinary.

In conclusion, the authors agree with Brown when he writes:

How one looks at theory makes a difference. If we limit our picture of theory to include only an ideal or hypothetical set of facts, principles, or circumstances, we are likely to perpetuate in our thinking the separation of theory from practice. We restrict theory to an ideal realm of abstract knowledge and unprovable assumptions which can be connected to the real world of practical affairs by nothing more substantial than mystical moonbeams. With theory thus idealized we assure ourselves of the failure in practice of what looked so promising in theory. On the other hand, if we can widen our thinking to permit theory to be seen as belief, policy, or proposed procedure to serve as a basis of action, we will be able to reunite theory and practice. Theory might then be seen as the intelligent explanation of practice, which permits theory to follow practice as well as lead it. Theory, in this broader view, is always developed in association with practice and serves as its frame of reference.[16]

So much for theory. Now see if any of the theory that you have learned helps you to reach decisions about what the teacher should do in the problem situations that follow.

References

Amidon, E., and Hunter, E. *Improving Teaching.* New York: Holt, Rinehart & Winston, 1966.

Biddle, B. J., and Ellena, W. J. *Contemporary Research on Teacher Effectiveness.* New York: Holt, Rinehart & Winston, 1964.

Brophy, J. E., and Good, T. L. *Teacher-Child Dyadic Interaction: A Manual for Coding Classroom Behavior.* University of Texas at Austin: Research and Development Center for Teacher Education, Report Series No. 27, December, 1969.

Brown, B. B. *The Experimental Mind in Education.* New York: Harper & Row, 1968.

Combs, A. W., and Snygg, D. *Individual Behavior.* New York: Harper & Row, 1959.

Dewey, J. *How We Think.* Boston: D. C. Heath, 1910.

Gordon, I. J., ed. *Criteria for Theories of Instruction.* Washington, D.C.: Association for Supervision and Curriculum Development, 1968.

Jackson, P. W. *Life in Classrooms.* New York: Holt, Rinehart & Winston, 1968.

Kilpatrick, W. H. *Remaking the Curriculum.* New York: Newsom, 1936.

Lindgren, H. C. *Educational Psychology in the Classroom.* 3rd ed. New York: Wiley, 1967.

McDonald, F. J. *Educational Psychology.* 2nd ed. Belmont, Calif.: Wadsworth, 1965.

Medley, D. M., and Mitzell, H. E. "Measuring Classroom Behavior by Systematic Observation." In *Handbook of Research on Teaching,* edited by N. L. Gage. Chicago: Rand McNally, 1963.

Perkins, H. V. *Human Development and Learning.* Belmont, Calif.; Wadsworth, 1969.

Rogers, C. R. *Client-Centered Therapy.* Boston: Houghton Mifflin, 1951.

Rosenthal, R., and Jacobson, L. *Pygmalion in the Classroom.* New York: Holt, Rinehart & Winston, 1968.

Skinner, B. F. *Contingencies of Reinforcement.* New York: Appleton-Century-Crofts, 1969.

---

[16]B. B. Brown, *The Experimental Mind in Education* (New York: Harper & Row, 1968), p. 8.

Chicken Little

Maple Grove Elementary, Junior High, and Senior High School, a modern brick complex connected by covered walkways and planted atriums, stands silhouetted against a dark, overcast sky on this morning in early October. The school, built in the 1950s, serves the small county seat of a basically agricultural county in a midwestern state. Children dressed in raincoats and boots are seen scurrying up the steps of the elementary school as heavy raindrops begin to fall.

Mrs. Grimes, the principal, stands at her office window alternately watching the arriving children and the quickly approaching storm. She is a pleasant-faced, somewhat stout woman of 50 with softly waved gray hair framing her face.

Mrs. Grimes: (Softly, under her breath) Chicken Little was right!

Mrs. James, a first-grade teacher, overhears her comment as she enters the principal's office to pick up some supplies before the last bell rings. Mrs. James is a trim, attractive young woman of 27 who has taught at Maple Grove Elementary for the past seven years. She received her B.A. degree from one of the state teachers colleges and her M.Ed. in Early Childhood from the state university. Her husband, Joel, is a secondary school biology teacher in the same complex. Mrs. James gathers up some construction paper and crosses to Mrs. Grimes.

Mrs. James: (Laughing) I could have sworn you said something about Chicken Little.

Mrs. Grimes: (Glancing up and smiling) Well, you've got to admit—the sky *is* falling in! Just look at those storm clouds off to our right.

Mrs. James joins her at the window and they watch great sheets of rain falling in the distance. A brilliant flash of lightning prompts both of them to move away from the window. Mrs. Grimes crosses to the files on her desk and picks out the permanent attendance record of Mrs. James' class.

Mrs. Grimes: (Opening the record) Nancy, I've been meaning to ask you about one of your students—Johnny Harrison. (She glances down at the record) I see here that he's been absent more than he's been present! What's the story on him?

Mrs. James: I really wish I knew. Johnny's absences are a mystery that I want to unravel with Mrs. Harrison soon. I thought I might set up a home visit with her next week to talk about Johnny. (She adds) Mrs. Harrison didn't come to our first scheduled parent-teacher conference this year. She works odd hours—which may be her reason.

Mrs. Grimes: Have you contacted our school nurse about Johnny?

Mrs. James: (Nodding) I did that the first week Johnny was absent. She's gone by his house twice to check on him and each time she says Johnny seems perfectly fit, but he complains of feeling sick at his stomach.

Mrs. Grimes: (With interest) What's he like in class when he does come? Does he create any disturbances? (She crosses behind her desk and sits down)

Mrs. James: (Continuing on a puzzled note) You'd think he would—particularly since he's so much bigger and older than the other children. But it's a funny thing . . . in class he's either crying—I mean, really sobbing like a baby—or he just sits absolutely depressed and apathetic.

Mrs. Grimes: (Glancing at her watch) We've got a few more minutes before you have to be back in the room. (Motioning Mrs. James to sit) Tell me a little more about this crying behavior. What seems to set it off?

Mrs. James: (Sitting on the edge of the chair with her hands clasped in front of her) Well, since the first day of school he starts screaming the minute his mother brings him to the door. He clings to her and sobs hysterically. It takes me hours to get him quieted down. Luckily I've Mrs. Browning as my aide this year, so she takes him into the rest room and tries to soothe him. Finally, Johnny seems to spend all his energy and allows himself to be led back into class by Mrs. Browning. The rest of the day he just sits morosely, usually in a chair away from the others. (She adds with concern) Sometimes, he gets out of his chair and just sits on the floor, for *hours,* with tears welling in his eyes; and Johnny sometimes just gets up from his seat and wanders out of the classroom, muttering, "I'm going home to see Mommy." I've had to go myself or send Mrs. Browning after him 8 or 10 times at least! (Shaking her head) I've never had a child like this before. (Reconsidering) Oh, I've had children who cried at the first of school because of the strangeness of it all or because of their initial reluctance to leave their mother. (She pauses for a moment) But that kind of behavior usually stops as soon as they get caught up in the class activities.

Mrs. Grimes: (Smiling) Nancy, I've seen you in operation too many times. I find it difficult to imagine *any* child not intrigued by all the exciting things going on in your room.

Mrs. James: (Thoughtfully) Not Johnny. He's such a pitiful child—I really don't know what to make of him. (Ruefully) And frankly, I don't seem to have any success with him at all. (She adds) This is his second year in the first grade, you know, and he just doesn't seem to learn anything. Why, he's never even learned the complete alphabet, and he still needs help writing his name. (The last bell interrupts her chain of thought) Oh, my goodness. It's time for all the children to be in the room. I'd better run. (Collecting her supplies, she starts toward the door) I'll let you know how I make out with Johnny's mother. Maybe she can shed some light on Johnny's problems.

Mrs. James enters her brightly lighted classroom and sees all the children clustered at the windows. Mrs. Browning, the aide, moves from group to group and talks to the children in soft tones. The children's faces are a study of contrasting fear and awe as they look at the ever-darkening sky and the deluge of rain. A deafening thunderclap sends most of the girls and a few of the boys to the protecting sides of Mrs. James and Mrs. Browning for comfort.

Cathy: (Holding her hands to her ears as she shrieks) Oh, Mrs, James, I'm scared!

Brenda: (Starting to cry) I'm scared, too. . . . I don't like thunder and lightning.

Mrs. James: (Soothingly) Girls and boys, why don't you gather round me and I'll tell you a story about a little boy who wanted to find out about lightning.

She motions the children to sit on the comfortable-looking hooked rug in the center of the room. She pulls a rocking chair over to the rug and sits in their midst. A few children continue to cast baleful looks over their shoulders at the stormy scene outdoors. One child still lingers at the window and he exclaims in a loud voice just as the rain reaches downpour proportions.

Charles: Teacher, teacher—here comes Johnny. Boy, is he getting wet!

The children, once more diverted to the rain outside, rush back to the windows. They see a car drive off and Johnny's stolid little figure move slowly to the school entrance. Johnny, wiping at his eyes, seems oblivious to the rain. Just as he is seen approaching the entrance to the building, another tremendous clap of thunder sounds. Johnny freezes and a look of anguish crosses his face. He turns and races back down the sidewalk after the departing car driven by his mother. The children in the classroom start shouting, "Johnny is running away!"

Suanne: Teacher, Johnny's out in the street and he's going to get run over by a car!

Mrs. James: (In a deliberately calm voice) Children, you stay with Mrs. Browning. I'm going to get Johnny. I won't be long. (With a nod to Mrs. Browning, who is already directing the children back to their places on the rug, Mrs. James rushes from the room)

Just as Mrs. James dashes from her room she encounters the principal in the hall. Without stopping she quickly relates over her shoulder in passing what's happened and asks Mrs. Grimes to call Johnny's mother. She hurries to the entrance and then sees a police car stopping at the curb. The policeman gets out of the car and walks around to the other side. He opens the door and picks up a sobbing Johnny and carries him up the sidewalk.

Policeman: I saw this boy running down the middle of the street, screaming at the top of his voice. I thought I'd better pick him up before he got hit by a car—it's so dark out there you can hardly see to drive.

He releases Johnny who then clings to Mrs. James. His shoes, socks, and pants are soaked and he presents a mournful, bedraggled, hang-dog appearance. Mrs. James takes his hand and leads him down the hall.

Thirty minutes later Mrs. James is showing a filmstrip to the children when there is a knock at the door. Mrs. James crosses to the door and greets Mrs. Harrison, a harried-looking woman with a pinched, concerned look on her face. Mrs. James turns momentarily back to Mrs. Browning and asks her to continue the lesson for her, and she then joins Mrs. Harrison in the hall.

Mrs. Harrison: I've brought some dry things for Johnny. I'll just leave them with you—because if he sees me, I'll *never* get away from him!

Mrs. James: Oh, I'm so glad you're here, Mrs. Harrison. (Motioning to the clothes) And thank you for bringing these by. Johnny got so drenched that I hated to see him sit all day in his wet clothing. (She takes the clothes from Mrs. Harrison) I'll just send Harry with Johnny to the rest room so Johnny can get into these dry things. (She gives the clothes to Mrs. Browning, whispers instructions to her, and quickly rejoins Mrs. Harrison)

Mrs. Harrison: (Turning to go) Well, I'd better go now. . . .

Mrs. James: (Earnestly) Oh, could you wait just a moment. I thought we might talk about Johnny.

Mrs. Harrison: (Reluctantly) Well, frankly, I don't have too much time. I had to get off from work to go home and get Johnny's clothes to bring here —so I've really got to get back.

Mrs. James: (Quickly) Yes, of course, I can understand that. (She adds) But would it be possible for us to talk this afternoon? (Mrs. Harrison is already shaking her head negatively) I'll stay here until you get off work and we can talk for a while. I'm very concerned about Johnny's absences.

Mrs. Harrison: (With resignation) Oh, well, I guess I might as well go on and talk now. One time is as inconvenient as another.

Mrs. James touches her arm in appreciation, murmurs "Good," and directs her to the nearby faculty lounge where they sit in a somewhat awkward silence.

Mrs. James: (Clearing her throat) Mrs. Harrison, I might as well be frank. I don't know what to make of Johnny. He's sick so often, and when he *is* here, he just doesn't seem to get involved with anything. He cries for such a long time after you leave—and then when he finally does stop crying, he just sits—just sits! (She unconsciously imitates his apathetic posture)

Mrs. Harrison: (Nodding) Yes, I know. Johnny's always been a nervous, fidgety, demanding child. And when his father and I were divorced two years ago he seemed to get even worse. (Half to herself) He never really seemed too close to his father, but I never will forget his, uh—(Searching for words) his *breakdown* when he saw his father packing to leave that last time. (Thoughtfully) Funny, his father's leaving scarcely bothered his younger brother at all (Continuing) But Johnny, that poor kid, grabbed at his father's legs as he was walking out the door. John—his father— got furious! He pushed Johnny down and called him a crazy kid—Johnny *was* acting crazy, too! Johnny crawled over to the door and started banging his head against the door, over, and over, and over. (Her voice trails off for a minute, then she resumes) Johnny seemed to get over his crying jags for awhile, but when I put him in kindergarten that year he'd cry so hard his stomach would be in knots! Finally I just had to take him out. Then last year I'd drop him off at school and I'd have to come get him before the hour was over. He'd throw up or gag until I got there—and I *had* to do something. (She spreads her hands in frustration) This year it's the very same thing. (Firmly) Frankly, I can't take much more.

Mrs. James: I can understand your feelings. He seems to be worse at the first of the week—on Mondays and Tuesdays.

Mrs. Harrison: Yes, he seems almost bearable on Fridays and over the weekend he plays with Charles, my 5-year-old, and the younger children in the apartment building where we live. But on Sunday he starts complaining of stomach cramps. By Monday morning he's pitiful—won't eat breakfast, threatens to throw up, and sobs all the way to school. I'm at my wit's end. (With a sigh) I've *got* to go to work—and he's got to go to school. That's all there is to it. But he *hates* school!

Mrs. James: What does Johnny do when he stays home?

Mrs. Harrison: (Plaintively) Well, first, I have to call in that I'm not going to be able to work that day. Then Johnny just lies down on the livingroom sofa and we watch television all day. Charles is in kindergarten, so Johnny and I are there by ourselves. Sometimes, I read to him or we play—usually with Charles' toys. (Firmly) But I get so frustrated not being able to get to my job! I'm not going to be able to hold it much longer at this rate.

Mrs. James: Could you possibly get a babysitter?

Mrs. Harrison: (With some sarcasm) Are you kidding? I've tried that route. Johnny throws a tantrum if I'm not there! Even my own mother refuses to keep him. (She adds) The doctor's no help. He says Johnny's got a nervous stomach—whatever that means—and he says that Johnny will just have to grow out of it. (Under her breath) If we live so long! (She looks at her watch) What else can I tell you—except that I'm getting awfully tired of being called from work to come get Johnny! (She gets up and starts to button her raincoat)

Mrs. James: Thank you for giving me your time, Mrs. Harrison; I see now how difficult it would have been for you to come to our parent-teacher conference.

Late that afternoon after the children have gone, Mrs. Grimes stops by Mrs. James' classroom.

Mrs. Grimes: Hello, Nancy. I noticed you and Mrs. Harrison talking in the teachers' lounge this morning after the episode with Johnny. Did you learn anything helpful?

Mrs. James: (With a sigh) Nothing more than I'd suspected. And I'm still confused about what to do with Johnny.

CUMULATIVE RECORD

Westwood Elementary School

Name:	Harrison, Johnny Bruce, Jr.	
Address:	330 King Apartments	**Former school:**
Father:	Harrison, John B.	**Date entered:** 8-30-68
Mother:	Harrison, Betty L.	**General health:** Poor
Siblings:	Harrison, Charles W. (5-19-64)	**Handicaps:** Nervous stomach
		Date of birth: 7-20-62
Home phone: 603-4717		**Age:** 7
Occupation: Insurance Salesman		
Occupation: Receptionist		

TEST RECORD

INTELLIGENCE TESTS:

	CA	MA	IQ	Date	Grade
California Test of Mental Maturity: Language					
Non-language		NO TEST SCORE OBTAINABLE			
Stanford-Binet		Child is uncooperative			

ACADEMIC RECORD

Record the year's average as A, B, C, D, or F:

	Grade 1	Grade 2	Grade 3	Grade 4	Grade 5	Grade 6
Reading	F					
English						
Writing	F					
Spelling	F					
Arithemtic	F					
Social Studies						
Science and Health						
Art	F					
Physical Education	F					
Industrial Arts						
Music						

Write *Below*, *Average*, or *Above* to indicate level of accomplishment:

Work Habits	Below
Soc. and Personal Devel.	Below

Questions—"Chicken Little"

1. How would you characterize Johnnys behavior? Disturbed? Neurotic? Psychotic? Psychosomatic? Retarded? Acting-out? What behavioral evidence do you have to support your position?
2. What home factors contribute to Johnny's behavior in school? How is Johnny's attitude toward school an expression of his feelings toward his parents?
3. What is the relationship between Johnny and his mother? In what ways does Johnny's mother reinforce his negative feelings about going to school? What kind of relationship would you predict exists between Johnny and his younger brother?
4. Is there such a thing as school phobia? What is separation anxiety? Do these terms relate to Johnny's problem?
5. The school has no test records on Johnny. How might a teacher make informal appraisals about Johnny's ability in the absence of a group or individual IQ or achievement test?
6. What role might a teacher take in relation to a child like Johnny? What avenues are open to her? How could she get Johnny interested in the activities of the class?

Standards, stigma, maturity, and motivation

Jan Smith, an attractive first-grade teacher, is in her second year of teaching. She is completing her first year at Lincoln Elementary School. She and her husband, Ben, moved to the community in the fall. Ben had completed his law degree and wanted to practice in a small town. Lincoln School serves a small, lower middle-class community in a midwestern state. Jan sits waiting in the office to talk with Mr. Johnson, the elderly principal who has been at Lincoln 22 years—since it was built. Mr. Johnson finishes his phone call and turns to Jan.

Mr. Johnson: (Leans forward) Jan, you really fit in here! Young teachers sometimes have problems since we are set in our ways here. (With emphasis) However, I have really been pleased with your teaching! I mean it; I'm not just saying it to make you feel good. The other teachers have been pleased, too. Especially the other two first-grade teachers. They tell me that you've given them some new ideas and that the three of you have worked like a team.

Jan: (Smiling in a warm manner) Thank you, Mr. Johnson. I do enjoy my teaching, and Miss Grayson and Mrs. Wilson have really helped me a great deal. They tell me what they are doing and explain why, but still give me the freedom to teach my way.

Mr. Johnson: (Leans back and becomes business-like) I wanted you to know that we appreciate your teaching—but I also wanted to go over this

May 10 promotion list you sent to the office. I see you promoted every child.

Jan: (Frowning and with emphasis) Is there anything wrong with promoting everybody?

Mr. Johnson: (Business-like but warmly) No, not necessarily. However, I do wonder if it's wise to promote Randy Duncan. I think Randy would be hopelessly lost in the second grade. He wouldn't be able to keep up and he would take up so much of his teacher's time that it wouldn't be fair to the other students. I looked at his classroom performance and it matched the impression I had formed by watching him on the playground.

Jan: (Speaks slowly, thoughtfully) I know there will be some difficulties if we promote Randy but I don't want to penalize Randy unjustly. You see, Mr. Johnson, I feel quite concerned about this. Maybe it's because I had a bad experience last year.

Mr. Johnson: What happened?

Jan: (Sighs, then continues slowly) Last year I taught in a school where the policy was to retain first graders if they couldn't read. I was really in a turmoil since I had just graduated and could still remember reading that students should seldom be retained and then only if the retention is clearly to the child's benefit. Kevin was very, very large for his age. He came from a family of "repeaters." Several older brothers and sisters had repeated grades. He was slow all year, even with all the extra help I gave him. I sent many letters to his parents asking them for a conference, but never once did they reply. It was almost as if Kevin's failure were expected—at least they were sure willing to accept his poor performance.

Mr. Johnson: Did you ever call them on the phone or go see them?

Jan: No.

Mr. Johnson: What kind of work did Kevin's parents do?

Jan: (Speaks slowly and thoughtfully) His father was a janitor at the university and I think the mother was a checker at a supermarket.

Mr. Johnson: What finally happened?

Jan: (Shakes her head negatively) Well, my principal looked at Kevin's work, his achievement test scores, etc., and told me to retain Kevin. I wrote the parents telling them that I was afraid I would have to hold Kevin back and still got no reply from them. I was forced to retain Kevin in the first grade. Earlier this year I received a letter from Kevin's teacher this year, who is a friend of mine. She told me about his poor attitude and classroom behavior. (With emphasis) At least last year he was cooperative and wanted to learn! (Shakes her head and bites her lip) She says he is much larger than the other kids and sticks out like a sore thumb. In fact, she says, she has heard some first graders say things like, "There goes that stupid Kevin Thompson! He flunked first grade." When I got that letter I felt like I had branded Kevin for life. Since then I have read a great deal about the bad effects that retention can have on students. (Firmly) And I'm convinced that it is a poor policy.

Mr. Johnson: (Sympathetic but business-like) Jan, I know how you feel. I still remember the first student I had to retain. Maybe Kevin should have been promoted to the second grade. However, you must remember that each child has to be considered individually.

Jan: Well, let's talk about Randy. (With exasperation) Why would it be good to retain him?

Mr. Johnson: Randy is the smallest boy in your room and from watching him on the playground, I know he has very poor coordination. He also seems to stay by himself and he apparently has no close friends or social skills. I think he's immature. Children who are behind other pupils physically and emotionally as well as academically often profit from retention.

Jan: (As she tears a Kleenex in two) But Mr. Johnson, I learned in college that repeaters make less academic progress than a promoted child of comparable academic ability.

Mr. Johnson: (Talks with a mixture of anger and uneasiness) Jan, this is different. This is the real world—it's not a theoretical case study. College professors don't have to deal with students who can't learn and their parents. We have to uphold standards. Unearned promotions cause students to develop unrealistic beliefs about the relationship between hard work and success. We have to face up to reality.

Jan: But doesn't repeating first grade tell a child that he is inferior? (She adds, earnestly) It also seems to me that some students would never reach a minimum level and never leave the first grade if we hold to our standards!

Mr. Johnson: (In a placating tone) Jan, I'm not saying that all children need to be retained. But when a young first grader doesn't learn to read and is also physically and socially immature, I think the child should be retained. Some children are motivated by being retained and it gives them a second chance to learn the material. We just have to be careful and see to it that retention doesn't become a stigma.

Jan: (Argumentatively, and with emotion) It's hard for me to see how Randy will be motivated by spending the first two months of school next year going through readiness activities. What he needs next year is for the second-grade teacher to start him in the reading primer so he can learn to read! He's ready to start the primer. If he repeats the first grade, he will be bored during readiness activities and fall behind when academics begin. It seems such a waste. He knows what sounds are about. He's ready to read.

Mr. Johnson: (Firmly) Some low achievers like Randy do profit from retention. However, I want to observe him in the classroom and see how he gets along when he works on his own. Then I want to see him in his reading group. (With some authority) We'll get together next week and make a final decision. In the meantime, think things over carefully. Don't let last year's experiences blind you. Look at the case objectively.

STUDENT INFORMATION SHEET
(Developed and filled in by teacher on each child, partly from cumulative record data)

Pupil: Randy Duncan
Birth date: 9-15-64
Age: 6
Metropolitan readiness test: Absent
Peabody picture vocabulary: Scored in the very low, normal range.

	Grading Periods			
	1	2	3	4
Language Arts	U	U	N	U
Spelling	N	U	U	N
Math	N	N	N	N
Science	S	N	N	N
Social Studies	S	S	S	S

(Grading scale: E=excellent, S=satisfactory, N=needs to improve, U=unsatisfactory)

Parent conference notes: Saw Mrs. Duncan on 10-4-70. She remarried (Mr. Duncan) a year ago. She works at an insurance office as a secretary and is two months pregnant. Mother reports that Randy talks about the coming baby a great deal. Randy has an older sister in the fourth grade. Mother doesn't seem greatly interested in Randy.

Comments: Grading Period 1—Quiet, immature, very small, cries easily, baby-talks excessively.

Grading Period 2—Sweet, cooperative child, just can't read. I thought he had a learning problem but he scored "low normal" on the Peabody test.

Grading Period 3—Cooperative, very immature, still some baby-talk, not good at sounds; however, he is showing some progress, has finished the second pre-primer, will probably finish the third pre-primer before school ends. However, he won't get to the primer.

Standards, stigma, maturity, and motivation **35**

Questions—"Standards, stigma, maturity, and motivation"

1. Does threat of failure motivate students to work harder? What type of student attitude does failure create? What type of student attitude does social promotion create? How does retention affect the student's self-concept?
2. In general, how do retained children perform the next year? Do some students benefit from retention? Which ones?
3. In what ways can non-promotion affect the social adjustment of pupils? Is retention per se an inevitable stigma? How can the "branding" effects of retention be reduced?
4. How important are the school's academic standards? Don't social promotion policies lower such standards and eventually cheapen the value of the diploma?
5. To what extent should parents be involved in promote-retain decisions?
6. To what extent should the student be involved in promote-retain discussions?
7. What does the term "stimulus bound" mean? To what extent are the past experiences of Mrs. Smith and Mr. Johnson influencing their present decision?
8. Should Randy be promoted? When should children be retained? When should they be promoted? What criteria should be applied?

Dirty Donna

Van Buren Elementary School is located in a middle-class attendance area in an eastern city of 8000 population. It is housed in a modern structure of gleaming glass and brick surrounded by a manicured lawn and a well-equipped playground area. Inside the building, large, bright classrooms can be seen on both sides of the spacious hallway.

In Mrs. Smith's third-grade classroom, children are seated at moveable desks arranged in horizontal rows as they work on an English assignment. Mrs. Smith, a young, well-dressed teacher with one year of experience, walks slowly about the room, stopping occasionally to help children with their work. One 8-year-old girl, Donna, is unkempt and slovenly in appearance. Her long, disheveled hair hangs in her eyes and she is clothed in a dress which is dirty, stained, torn, and far too large. Donna is fidgeting in her chair. The teacher stops by Donna's desk, glances briefly at her paper, and then calls the class to attention.

Mrs. Smith: Class, I see you've all finished your work. Donna, will you please go to the board and explain to the other boys and girls how you marked the ninth group of words.

Donna gets out of her seat quickly and moves toward the front of the room. She bumps into Mark's desk, causing his paper to fall to the floor. Immediately she stoops to pick the paper up and places it on his desk. The class laughs as Mark holds his nose and leans away from Donna. Donna looks disconcerted, but she proceeds to the board where she completes the work correctly.

Mrs. Smith: That's fine, Donna. Now please choose someone else to have a turn.

Donna looks temporarily puzzled. Not knowing the names of the rest of the students, she reddens, pauses, and then points to Paul in the front row.

Kevin: (Snickering, holding his nose, and speaking in a low voice) Paul and Donna, Paul and Donna. . . .

Paul frowns and goes to the blackboard. Before he completes the work the bell rings. The children gather their books and jackets and walk in companionable groups of twos and threes to the cafeteria. Donna is the last to leave the room, and she is alone. She smiles hesitantly at Mrs. Smith as she walks by the teacher's desk.

As Mrs. Smith prepares to leave the room, John Morrison's mother comes into the classroom.

Mrs. Morrison: (Hands Mrs. Smith a note which reads: "You are a shitass. Donna") My husband and I were greatly distressed when John brought home this note yesterday and said that one of the girls who sat beside him in class had passed it to him. We certainly didn't think that he would be exposed to this kind of language in the third grade!

Mrs. Smith: I'm sorry this happened. I can readily appreciate your disapproval. I didn't realize that this kind of thing was going on. I see that Donna's name is at the bottom—I'll speak to her.

Mrs. Smith and Donna are alone in the classroom after school. Mrs. Smith sits at her desk while Donna stands just to the left of Mrs. Smith's chair.

Mrs. Smith: Donna, I asked you to wait for a few minutes after school so that we could talk about this note. (She hands the note to Donna, who takes it casually) Did you write this note and give it to John?

Donna: (Grinning) Yes.

Mrs. Smith: Donna, you want the children in your room to like you, don't you?

Donna: (Shrugging her shoulders) Sure.

Mrs. Smith: They won't think that you're a very nice little girl if you use words like these. Now, promise me that you won't do this again.

Donna: (Nodding) Okay!

It is several days later. Most of the students are working quietly at their desks using rulers to construct a set of number lines. Donna sits in a reading group of six students. Mrs. Smith calls on Donna. Although Donna has her book open and is seemingly concentrating on the lesson, another student has to help her find the place. Her reading is slow, jerky, and without expression. Consistently, she misses words on the second-grade level. Despondently, Donna finishes, picks up a ruler from the desk, and begins to poke her neighbors.

Mrs. Smith: Donna, quit distracting the other children. That ruler is not to be used for poking.

Donna smiles widely. The children seated near her turn away from her in aggravation. Mrs. Smith finishes with the reading group and sends the children back to their regular seats. She begins to walk around the room, pausing now and then to help the children with the number lines they are constructing. Suddenly, she hears a commotion in the back of the room. Children are moving their desks away from Donna as they whisper loudly about the odor. Mrs. Smith notices that Donna is in tears.

Mrs. Smith: Donna, what's wrong?
Donna: (Sobbing) I had a bad accident!

Donna had urinated and defecated. Mrs. Smith asks one of the boys to find the janitor and calls one of the girls aside.

Mrs. Smith: Mary, would you take Donna to the girls' room and help her clean up. She's awfully upset.

With reluctance Mary accompanies the sobbing Donna to the rest room, while Mrs. Smith leads the class to the library for the remaining 20 minutes of the day.

It is parent-teacher conference night and Donna's mother appears for the conference, wearing an unpressed blouse and ill-fitting, faded slacks. Mrs. Walker's strong odor compels Mrs. Smith to move back a few steps upon greeting her. Mrs. Smith sits at her desk and Mrs. Walker sits in a chair in front of the desk.

Mrs. Walker: (In a whining voice) First, you better let me explain why Donna wasn't at school yesterday. She lost her shoes in the morning, and then I couldn't get her to go in the afternoon. We got eight kids and the farm to take care of, and it's hard to keep track of all of them. Besides that, my husband works half the night as a machine operator at the factory. (Mrs. Walker pauses, sniffs, and wipes her nose with the back of her hand) That is, when he ain't sick or something.

Mrs. Smith: I understand. I thought we might talk tonight about Donna's progress. Although the IQ score from the first grade shows Donna to be about average, she was over a year below her grade level on our achievement test. I just don't believe Donna is doing as well in school as she could if she had some additional help at home.

Mrs. Walker: Well, my husband and me are so busy the kids just have to help each other with work.

Mrs. Smith: Mrs. Walker, would it be possible for you and your husband to take Donna to the library from time to time? She really needs more practice and encouragement in reading.

Mrs. Walker: Now, she don't need to go to the library to read. We've got some books at home . . . and besides, she don't want to do nothing but watch TV anyway.

Mrs. Smith: There is something else that I feel I need to discuss with you, Mrs. Walker. (She shows Mrs. Walker several notes) Donna has admitted to sending these around the room. I've spoken with her, but she continues. I'm sure you disapprove. Could you speak with her about them?

Mrs. Walker: (With a sheepish expression) Oh, I've told Donna time and time again that she shouldn't ought to repeat them things at school 'cause people wouldn't think she was very nice. Well, of course, she hears Bill and me use them words, but it's just natural at home.

Mrs. Smith: (Hesitantly) Mrs. Walker, I have to be frank about one other thing. The other children don't accept Donna as much as I'd like them to because of her body odor. She's such a pretty little girl and should have more friends, but the other children think she's dirty. (Mrs. Walker starts to cry)

Mrs. Smith appears uncomfortable as Mrs. Walker gets to her feet and stumbles out without another word.

Mrs. Smith: (Calling after Mrs. Walker) Wait, Mrs. Walker, please. . . .

Mrs. Smith, the guidance counselor, and the school nurse are seen seated around the counselor's desk in the guidance office.

Mrs. Smith: So, you see, Tom, that's the way the parent-teacher conference went. I'm so upset that I may have alienated Mrs. Walker. She seemed, outwardly at least, to be interested in her child's welfare. Now she may never come back for another conference!

Guidance Counselor: (Nodding) Sue, I can appreciate your concern. I've been interested in this family myself for some time. Just last week I paid a visit to the home and was even invited to stay for dinner. You'd find it hard to believe the living conditions there! Barnyard animals were in the house . . . on the table . . . in the beds; clothing and food were strewn all over the floor; some of the younger children were playing in their own filth. I have to confide to you—I had this overwhelming desire to wash my hands. I made some lame excuse not to stay and I left. And I did stop to wash my hands at a nearby filling station before returning to school!

School Nurse: I've been in that home, too, and it's just as bad as you describe. Every child in that family has lice. Poor Donna has the worse case I've ever seen . . . it's that long, lank hair of hers that makes her case so bad. She'll have to be out of school at least another week.

Mrs. Smith: I suspected that. Of course, every child in my class knows the reason for Donna's absence. Even before this, if Donna even so much as passed out papers, the other children drew away and blew at their papers as if to get rid of the dirt. Donna usually just blushes at their rebuffs, but her movements are becoming increasingly awkward. She looks so uncomfortable, poor thing.

School Nurse: I noticed something about Donna's mouth the other day. The whole area around her mouth is red and crusted. It wasn't an infection; it just looked raw.

Mrs. Smith: I think I can explain that. Invariably when Donna feels uncomfortable or anxious her tongue begins to circle the area around her mouth. Then that area reddens and crusts over. (Pausing, then earnestly) I want so to help her. What can I do?

Van Buren Elementary School

Name:	Walker, Donna Ann	Home phone:	None
Address:	Rt. #2, Box 1053	Occupation:	Machinist, Van Buren Tool Co.
Father:	Walker, William R.	Occupation:	Housewife
Mother:	Walker, Agnes P.		

Former school:	
Date entered:	8-30-66
General health:	Good
Handicaps:	None
Date of birth:	8-10-60
Age:	8

Siblings:

William R., Jr., Age 16   Michael S., Age 10
Sarah R., Age 14   Alma E., Age 6
Martha A., Age 13   Thomas A., Age 2
Mary B., Age 11

INTELLIGENCE TESTS:
California Test of Mental Maturity: Language
       Non-language

TEST RECORD

	CA	MA	IQ	Date	Grade
5-10-67	6-9	6-6	97	5-7-67	1
5-18-68	6-9	6-12	104		
	6-9	6-9	100		

ACHIEVEMENT TEST:
Stanford Achievement Test:

Grade	Word reading	Paragraph meaning	Spelling	Word st. skills	Arithmetic	Vocab.
1	1.0	−1.0	1.4	1.2	1.1	−1.0
2	1.3	−1.0	1.2	1.3		

Grade	Language		Science & Social Studies concepts	Arithmetic comp.	Arithmetic concepts	
2	−1.0		−1.0	1.4	1.1	

ACADEMIC RECORD

	1	2	3	4	5	6
Grade Level						
Citizenship	3	1				
Reading	3	2				
English						
Spelling		2				
Writing	3	2				
Social Studies						
Arithmetic	2	2				
Science						

KEY:
1. Child is working below grade level.
2. Child is working below grade level, but is making progress.
3. Child is working at grade level.
4. Child is doing excellent work at grade level.
5. Child is working above grade level.

Questions—"Dirty Donna"

1. What is social class and what are the differences between the social classes?
2. To what social class does Donna belong? Why?
3. What values does Donna seem to hold about (A) Dirty language? (B) Cleanliness?
4. What values does Mrs. Smith seem to hold about the above topics? Does Donna reject Mrs. Smith's values?
5. What does deprived mean? In what ways is Donna deprived?
6. What role has the home situation played in causing Donna to behave the way that she does in school?
7. How have Donna's peers in school affected her behavior?
8. How does Donna probably see herself? Why?
9. Do the home and the school seem to be meeting Donna's security needs? Why?
10. How do you explain the apparent inconsistency between Donna's IQ score on the one hand and her achievment test score and grades on the other?
11. Does the school's curriculum seem meaningful to Donna? Why?
12. Can and should the school do onything about the forces affecting Donna's behavior?

Brett the brat

It is almost 9:00 A.M. on a cool October day in New England. Suzanne Landers, a pretty, slender young 21-year-old girl with long, ash-brown hair is seen approaching the Elm Street Elementary School. Miss Landers is a senior in elementary education at the state university located in this small upstate, rural community with a population of 7600 people. She is to begin today an eight-week internship with Mrs. Mayes, a third-grade teacher who has been with this school for 23 years.

As Suzanne nears the school, she pauses for a moment to observe her surroundings. The freshly painted, two-story elementary school with white columns was built in 1936. It sits on a slight rise on a well-landscaped lawn.

Suzanne half runs up the steps and enters the front entrance. She proceeds to the office where she is met by the school secretary.

Mrs. Adams: (Cheerfully) Good morning. May I help you?

Suzanne: Yes, I'm Suzanne Landers. I'm to intern under Mrs. Mayes this fall. Could you tell me where her room is?

Mrs. Adams: Yes, I'll be happy to. (She comes to the door and holds it open for Suzanne to pass through) Mrs. Mayes' room is on the second floor. I'll take you there.

The rooms which line the hall are decorated with posters, pictures, and heavily decorated bulletin boards. The furniture is old, but not shabby. In each room the students are seen busily working at their desks as their teacher moves about the room from student to student. As they climb the stairs to the second floor, Suzanne and Mrs. Adams talk quietly.

Mrs. Adams: This is a nice school to work in. Students really seem to respect the teachers. We don't have very many problems here—our principal won't put up with any troublemakers for long. (She concludes proudly)

Suzanne: (Somewhat puzzled) It certainly is *quiet*. Somehow, I expected a little more activity. . . .

Her voice trails off as Mrs. Adams stops at Room 114. She and Mrs. Adams stand quietly as Mrs. Mayes, the third-grade teacher, acknowledges their presence with a nod. Mrs. Mayes, gazing around the room filled with 35 young children seated at their desks in long, horizontal rows, sees no disorder. Then she gives a warning look to her students as she brings her fingers to her lips in a "shush" gesture before she walks to the door to greet Suzanne and Mrs. Adams.

Mrs. Mayes: (Pleasantly) You must be Miss Landers from the University. I expected you earlier, but I guess you had no way of knowing our daily schedule. (Then to Mrs. Adams) Thank you, Claire. (Mrs. Adams smiles and leaves)

Suzanne: (With a nervous laugh) I'm sorry to be late . . . I . . . thought I'd get a ride but at the last minute I decided to walk . . . and. . . .

Mrs. Mayes: (Briskly) Let's go back to the children. (She pauses and says matter-of-factly) I believe it's customary for you interns to observe for a few days before you take the class; is that right?

Without waiting for an answer she directs her attention back to her class where a disturbance is taking place. Mrs. Mayes snaps her fingers twice in an attempt to get order, but she finds this unsuccessful in lessening the noise from the back of the room. She steps back into the room and sees two boys punching at each other. Mrs. Mayes moves quickly to separate them.

Mrs. Mayes: (Firmly, as she pulls the boys apart) Boys, boys, this must stop, *now!* I won't have this! (The boys briefly struggle to free themselves, but Mrs. Mayes has them in a firm grip) Now tell me what happened!

Joe: (Plaintively) Mrs. Mayes, I didn't do anything. Brett tripped me as I started to go to the pencil sharpener.

Mrs. Mayes nods, releases her hold, and motions him to his seat. She turns her attention to Brett, now squirming in her grasp.

Brett: (Grinning) Mrs. Mayes, I didn't mean to trip him. He just stumbled over my foot and. . . . (He is interrupted by an angry yank at his collar by Mrs. Mayes) Hey, don't do that! (He draws back his arm as if to strike her, but he is stopped by her menacing look)

Mrs. Mayes: Brett, I've told you before about fighting in school. Come with me, young man. (She takes him by the arm as if to lead him to the front of the room)

Brett: (Twisting away from her) I told you! Don't do that.

He begins to flail out against Mrs. Mayes and one or two blows fall on her arms. Mrs. Mayes succeeds in grabbing his arms and holding him securely. She maneuvers over to the intercom and presses the button connecting her to the office. The class sits in numb silence as she speaks into the intercom.

Mrs. Mayes: (With authority) It's Brett Browning again—fighting in class. Ask Mr. Thompson to come down, please. (Turning to Brett) Brett, how many times do you have to be spanked before you learn not to fight in school?

A few minutes later Mr. Thompson, the portly 53-year-old principal, appears at the door and motions Mrs. Mayes, still holding Brett, to accompany him. Mrs. Mayes moves to leave and she motions Suzanne to take over in her absence. Suzanne looks after her for a long pause, shrugs her shoulders imperceptibly, and moves to the front of the desk facing the subdued students.

Suzanne: (Hesitantly) Boys and girls, I'm Miss Landers, your intern teacher this fall, and I'll be with you until January 16. I, ah (She pauses with uncertainty), I don't have anything planned, so why don't we just chat for a few minutes until Mrs. Mayes and Brett return, okay? (Her friendly smile seems to break the ice and the children begin to talk all at once)

Jo Ann: (A pert little 8-year-old in the front) Brett's going to get another spanking. He's not nice.

Tom: (A tall boy in the back) Brett gets a spanking 'bout every day.

The other children nod and smile in affirmation as though they are pleased. Mrs. Mayes then appears at the door and Suzanne walks toward the back of the room and takes a seat to observe, sighing with relief.

Mrs. Mayes and Suzanne sit talking quietly together at the end of the school day.

Mrs. Mayes: (Wearily) I'm sorry that you had to see Brett's terrible behavior on your very first day, but I must admit, it's typical for him! He's an impossible child! (She makes a deprecatory gesture)

Suzanne: (With interest) Tell me a little more about him, won't you?

Mrs. Mayes: (Offhandedly) Oh, he's bright, there's no doubting that. *That* may be part of his problem. He's a smart aleck, if you know what I mean. (She continues) I heard about him when he was still in the first grade. Evidently he could read before coming to school and he would laugh out loud when other children in his reading group would mispronounce words. Mrs. Johnston, his first-grade teacher—she's one of my best friends—said he was an unpopular child, primarily because the other children resented his constant correction of their errors. He seemed to delight in making the others feel inferior to him.

Suzanne: Does he still do that to the other children?

Mrs. Mayes: (With heat) Constantly! He belittles the others, even the really competent ones. Yet, when *he* makes a mistake he can't stand criticism. If another child points out Brett's error, then Brett gets absolutely rigid, glares at him, and yells, "Liar!" (She nods her head) And before you know it, Brett has found some way to physically attack the other child. Then, once he's got it out of his system, he just grins and tries to look innocent. He's hopeless.

Suzanne: (Caught up in the conversation) Do you usually send him to the principal for this aggressive behavior?

Mrs. Mayes: Well, frankly, I've gotten to the stage where I just want to get him out of the room. The first of the year I must have spanked him every day of the week. Now he's gotten so bad—you saw him hit me today—that I can't cope with him. (With finality) I'd much rather the principal deal with Brett. He's the only one who can handle him.

Suzanne: What about sending Brett to a school counselor? Might that help?

Mrs. Mayes: (Laughing) Oh, are you idealistic! Let me tell you about Brett. His father's a dentist and his mother holds a master's degree in sociology. They've given that child everything. He had a chemistry set when he was four. And they fully equipped a three-room playhouse with handmade miniature furniture at the back of their house just for him. The whole town was amazed at the money that cost! (Thoughtfully) But at the same time Brett's parents really don't pamper him. Why, I've seen his father jerk him out of his seat for acting up in a restaurant and spank him hard in front of everyone. (Firmly) Brett doesn't need a counselor— he's not emotionally disturbed. He's just a hateful, ill-tempered little boy who needs to know he can't get away with murder. (She adds) You saw how quiet the other children were with Brett out of the room. If you're wise, you'll follow my advice and let him know you mean business right from the start.

Suzanne: (Hesitantly) Mrs. Mayes, my teachers stressed over and over again that we should not physically punish the child, that we should. . . .

Mrs. Mayes: (Interrupting Suzanne's point) Yes, I've heard all that before. (She pats Suzanne's hand as she gathers some papers and a class roll from her desk) Miss Landers, I suspect you have a lot to learn.

She takes Suzanne's arm to guide her toward the door. Suzanne, with a puzzled, intense look on her face, walks slowly along beside Mrs. Mayes.

It is the morning of Suzanne's first day of intern teaching. For the past week she has been observing in the back of the classroom.

Suzanne bustles nervously around the room, stopping occasionally to straighten a picture on the bulletin board or to align the venetian blinds. Mrs. Mayes is at the back of the room grading papers. She glances up from time to time and smiles to herself.

The bell rings, and as the children begin to enter the classroom, Suzanne takes her place close to the door, smiles and begins to greet them by name.

One student: (Whispering to another) Look, Mis Landers is going to teach us today. Isn't that good? I like her. She's pretty.

Then the child, seeing Mrs. Mayes in the back of the room, cuts off her conversation and goes to her desk. The children take their seats quietly and sit whispering together. Several of them smile warmly at Suzanne. They all look up hushed and expectant as she begins to speak.

Suzanne: (Brightly) Good morning, boys and girls. Today is the first day I'm going to be with you as your teacher. I was busy all last week learning your names and the schedule, but I'm still a little shaky. You'll have to help me out. Will you? (She smiles at the children, and they return her smile and nod their heads in affirmation) All right, children, let's begin our spelling lesson, shall we?

It is later that morning. Suzanne appears poised and confident as she concludes the spelling lesson and directs the children to prepare for reading from their basal texts. The children are cooperative and relaxed and without a murmur they smoothly make the transition from their work in spelling to reading. They now sit quietly with their reading books open, awaiting Suzanne's instructions.

Suzanne: I'm pleased to see such good scores on your spelling tests this morning. Now, let's turn our attention to our story, "They Didn't Believe Jake." I want you all to read the whole story silently.

The children seem absorbed by the story. Suzanne walks slowly around the room, pausing from time to time to interpret a word or phrase. Finally, all the students seem to have finished the story and Suzanne, standing by the window, begins to talk about it.

Suzanne: Sometimes parents just don't seem to believe what their children say. Have you ever had *your* parents fail to understand what you say and what you feel? (There is a loud chorus of yeses)

Suzanne: (Continuing in a friendly, conversational tone) Let's read between the lines in our story. I mean, let's imagine what Jake must be feeling when nobody believes him. It's not written down, but we can put ourselves in Jake's place, can't we?

Ann: (Eagerly) I think Jake must have been sad, and maybe he cried.

Brett: (From the back of the room) That's stupid! Boys don't cry! (He laughs loudly in derision; a few other boys laugh too)

Suzanne: (Surprised at this first outburst of the day from Brett) Brett, you have a point. Perhaps boys don't cry so much as girls do, but Ann might be right, too.

Brett: (Persisting) Ann's a crybaby. She thinks everyone's a baby like she is. (Under his breath) She's stupid!

Suzanne: (Ignoring his last comment) What do some of the others think Jake must have felt? Yes, Charles. (She nods to a bespectacled little boy in the front row)

Charles: Jake thought they didn't trust him. I'll bet he wouldn't tell his parents any more things after that.

Suzanne: (Nodding) Yes, I can see how Jake might do just that.

Brett: (Without waiting for recognition blurts out) Jake would feel mad at his parents. And he'd just tell them he didn't care what they felt. If they didn't believe him, he'd just tell them they were dummies!

Sally: (Shaking her head) You're not supposed to call your Mother and Daddy dummies.

Brett: (Loudly) That's silly. If they're dummies, they're dummies!

His voice rises on a shrill note. Suzanne is nonplussed by this final outburst. She stands almost helpless for a minute, obviously puzzled at what to do next.

Mrs Mayes: (Angrily rising to her feet at the back of the room) Well, I've heard enough, young man. (She grabs his arm and jerks him toward the door) This has gone quite far enough! You need a good paddling for this. (She jerks him a step further) Come along, right now. You're going to the principal with me. (Brett pulls back, but Mrs. Mayes forces him to accompany her)

It is late afternoon of the same day. The children have gone and Suzanne stands pensively at the window. She looks up as Mrs. Mayes enters the room.

Mrs. Mayes: I'm sorry about having to take over this morning, but I felt that things had gone too far.

Suzanne: That's all right. (Hesitantly) I . . . I was just caught off guard, I guess.

Mrs. Mayes: (With some kindness) You should never have let it go so far. (Then, firmly) *Now,* do you see what I mean by firmness with Brett? The only thing he respects is a good paddling.

Suzanne: (Earnestly) It's just not my way, Mrs. Mayes. I just don't like the thought of striking a child.

Mrs. Mayes: Then, tell me, my dear, how else could you have handled it?

CUMULATIVE RECORD

Elm Street Elementary School

Name:	Browning, Brett Jeremy	**Former school:**	
Address:	224 Maple Drive	**Date entered:**	8-30-66
Father:	Browning, Robert Brett	**General health:**	Good
Mother:	Browning, Doris J.	**Handicaps:**	None
Siblings:	None	**Date of birth:**	7-24-60
		Age:	8

Home phone: 734-0738
Occupation: Dentist
Occupation: Sociologist

TEST RECORD

INTELLIGENCE TESTS:
California Test of Mental Maturity:

	CA	MA	IQ	Date	Grade
Language	6-9	8-11	133	5-14-67	1
Non-language	6-9	8-9	129		

ACADEMIC RECORD

Grade Level	1	2	3	4	5	6
Citizenship	1	1				
Reading	5	5				
English						
Spelling		5				
Writing	5	5				
Social Studies						
Arithmetic	5	5				
Science						

KEY:
1. Child is working below grade level.
2. Child is working below grade level, but is making progress.
3. Child is working at grade level.
4. Child is doing excellent work at grade level.
5. Child is working above grade level.

Questions—"Brett the brat"

1. How would you describe the technique that Mrs. Mayes used to deal with Brett's behavior? How effective was it? How should Suzanne deal with Brett?
2. What is discipline and what is its goal? What does Mrs. Mayes' goal seem to be as far as Brett is concerned? What is preventive discipline? What are some methods which might be considered preventive discipline?
3. How effective is the technique of planned ignoring that Redl refers to in his book, *The Aggressive Child*?
4. How important is the establishment of limits in a disciplinary situation? How does a teacher establish limits?
5. Would there be any advantage in having students help formulate the rules in the classroom? How could this be accomplished?
6. What home factors seem to contribute to Brett's classroom behavior?
7. What relationships seem to exist between Brett and his peers? Could the teacher use the peer group to bring about changes in Brett's behavior?
8. Do you agree with Mrs. Hayes that Brett doesn't need the services of a counselor?
9. How effective is punishment in changing a child's behavior? Are such changes usually permanent? What are some of the different kinds of punishment that teachers use? How effective are rewards in changing pupil behavior? Do rewards have to be material things like candy or gold stars? What is the most effective way to use rewards?
10. How would you deal with a belligerent, aggressive, actively resistant child? How would you deal with passive resistance?

The eternal triangle: teacher, pupil, parent

Joan Purcell, a 27-year-old fourth-grade teacher, has taught at Mt. Summit for five years. Mt. Summit is an exclusive elementary school in a west coast community of 400,000. The children who attend Mt. Summit come from upper middle- to upper-class professional homes. Joan and the fifth-grade teacher, Mary Steinkle, are sitting in Joan's classroom discussing an impending teacher-parent conference.

Joan: (Wrinkles her face as she nervously looks at her watch and sighs) Ten minutes after 3:00, they'll be here in 20 minutes.

Mary: Good grief, Joan. You're blowing this thing out of proportion. I know you don't hold many teacher-parent conferences but. . . .

Joan: (In exasperation) But Tim's mother is *only* an officer in the PTA and his father is *only* one of the most influential lawyers in town. And I have to tell them that I think that they are placing too much emphasis on Tim's school achievement.

Mary: (Her surprise is evident) Say, I didn't know you had a problem with Tim. I don't know him well but he seems like a polite, compliant student. When you said you had a conference with the Baileys, I thought they were coming in for a friendly visit. They come to all PTA meetings, talk a lot, and seem to be interested in school, and I thought. . . .

Joan: No, I called them and asked them to come in for a visit.

Mary: (Hesitantly) What's the problem?

Joan: Well, you put your finger on it a moment ago when you described Tim as a polite, compliant student. The point is he's too compliant. I think he's a frightened little boy who works slavishly for high grades because his whole self-concept is tied to his school achievement. A good grade is his only acceptable proof of being a good, worthwhile person.

Mary: (Apologetically) I'm sorry for my flippant comments. You aren't going to have an easy conference. (She adds) How did you draw these conclusions about Tim?

Joan: I first became aware of Tim's need for good grades through his clinging dependency upon me. During the first few days of school when I gave class assignments, Tim would constantly come to my desk for clarification and assurance—"What do you want us to do, Miss Purcell? Where can I find the answer? Is this right?" He constantly demanded that I approve his work. (She admits) At first I was flattered by his heavy reliance. It's nice to be needed; but gradually it occurred to me that his dependence was too excessive—it wasn't normal!

Mary: Why did you wait until now, in April, to talk with the Baileys, if Tim's behavior was so disturbing to you?

Joan: Well, I thought I could deal with Tim in the classroom. In fact (She smiles broadly), I was relatively successful in getting him to work on his own.

Mary: How so?

Joan: I wanted to reduce his reliance on me so I first shifted our meetings to his seat. When he came to my desk, I would send him back to his desk and immediately follow him and thank him for being in his seat working on the problem. However, at first it didn't work. I would help him at his desk and then leave, but he would be right back at my desk a few minutes later, and we would have to go through the whole process again.

Mary: How did you solve the problem?

Joan: Well, in time I learned that after I helped him at his seat, I needed to keep him there. So I would tell him something like—"Well, now we've worked the first one, you work on the next three and I will be back in 10 minutes to go over the work with you." Then I would come back in a couple of minutes and praise him for being in his seat, and so on.

Mary: (Teasingly) Hey, you're a behavior modifier! That guy at school must have made some impression on you. What else did you do?

Joan: (With a flushed face) Oh, not much. I gradually delayed going back to his desk 15 minutes, then 30 minutes, etc. I also forced him to evaluate his own work before I graded it; I wanted him to express his feelings about his own work. I wanted him to learn that his work can be good before I placed a red A on it. I've seen progress in his private relations with me but in public contacts in front of the class he is still the same frightened, compulsive student with his strong need to comply with my every request.

Mary: (Puzzled) What do you mean? What does this compulsive, strong need look like?

Joan: When I ask Tim a question in class, I feel like a traffic light. He examines my face intently looking for clues that suggest how he should respond. If I nod my head or signal approval in any way as he answers, he proceeds rapidly, speaking faster and louder. But at my slightest sign of disapproval he quickly changes the direction of his answer. The sad thing is that he acts this way even when he's answering questions that have no right answers. I remember one day I asked him if he would like to be an astronaut. As he was describing how much fun it would be, I shook my head slightly at a student sitting behind him who had his hand up. After I shook my head, Tim suggested that the job might get boring after a while. (She pauses, then adds earnestly) Mary, I think he's paying too high a price for his good grades. He'll do anything to get them. It's all he thinks about.

Mary: Why did you call his parents?

Joan: I'm reaching out, Mary; but I think Tim's parents contribute to his problem. My guess is that they stress his school achievement too much and that they let him know that he is good only after he does something well. Almost telling him that they like him only when he performs well.

Mary: You'd better be careful. How are you going to bring that up in the conference?

Joan: I don't know. I just plan to talk about his compulsive behavior in class and hope that we can get to the home some way. I'm just going to play it by ear.

Mary: Play it by ear! You'd better think about this some more. How come you're so sure that his parents act that way?

Joan: I'm not sure. It's just a hunch, but I have had a few conversations with Tim about what he likes to do at home and, well, let me show you this. (She hands a sheet to Mary) A few days ago I had the children respond to this sentence-completion interest inventory that I made up. I'm not qualified to really interpret these things but I do know Tim's responses are not like other fourth-grade boys' responses.

Mary: (Briefly glances at the sheet and hands it back to Joan) I don't put much stock in these things and I don't think you should either. Say, it's 3:30. I'd better clear out of here. You'll see me first thing tomorrow. I want to know what happens. Good luck!

Ten minutes later Mr. and Mrs. Bailey arrive. Their attractive physical appearance and expensive clothing give them a strong presence and Joan feels like a nervous child.

Joan: Good afternoon, Mr. and Mrs. Bailey. I'm glad we have this chance to visit and talk about Tim.

Mr. Bailey: (Quickly) What's wrong with Tim, Miss Purcell? Has he done something wrong?

1. My father likes me best: When I bring home an A paper and when I finish my homework.

2. My mother likes me best: When my room is perfectly straight.

3. I feel proudest: When I get all A's.

4. When I finish school I want to be:

5. My favorite hobby is: Reading.

6. When I go home in the afternoon I like to: Finish my homework.

7. My worst fear is: Get poor marks.

8. People are happiest:

9. My friends: Are quiet.

10. My favorite school subject is:

11. School is: Hard work.

CUMULATIVE RECORD

Mt. Summit Elementary School

Name:	Bailey, Timothy L.		
Address:	529 Booth Avenue	Home phone:	844-8464
Father:	Bailey, Thomas J.	Occupation:	Lawyer
Mother:	Bailey, Ruth	Occupation:	Housewife (holds a teaching certificate)
Siblings:	None		

Former school:
Date entered: 8-29-66
General health: Excellent
Handicaps: None
Date of birth: 9-1-60
Age: 9

TEST RECORD

INTELLIGENCE TESTS:
California Test of Mental Maturity:

	CA	MA	IQ	Date	Grade
Language	6-0	6-0	100	9-15-66	1
Non-language	6-0	6-8	113		
	6-0	6-4	106		

ACHIEVEMENT TEST:
Stanford Achievement Test:

Grade	Word reading	Paragraph meaning	Spelling	Word st. skills	Arithmetic	Vocab.
1	2.5	3.0	2.7	2.2	3.1	3.0

5-10-67

ACADEMIC RECORD

Record the year's average as A, B, C, D, or F:

	Grade 1	Grade 2	Grade 3	Grade 4	Grade 5	Grade 6
Reading	A	A	A			
English			A			
Writing	A	A	A			
Spelling	A	A	A			
Arithmetic	A	A	A			
Social Studies			A			
Science and Health			B+			
Art	A	A	A			
Physical Education	B	C	C			
Music	B+	A−	B+			

Questions—"The eternal triangle: teacher, pupil, parent"

1. From the available evidence, would you draw the same conclusions about Tim that Joan did? Should she have gathered more evidence before asking Tim's parents to come in for a conference?
2. What is compulsivity? How does it differ from anxiety?
3. How would you define an over-achieving student? Is over-achieving a good student characteristic? How would you define the compulsively over-achieving student?
4. What is need achievement? What family rearing practices and parental values are associated with the development of high need achievement?
5. How Does Tim probably see himself? What relationships exist between self-concept and academic achievement? How does the self-concept change?
6. What is behavior modification? Should teachers modify behavior? Evaluate Miss Purcell's strategy for increasing Tim's classroom autonomy. How would you improve upon her strategy?
7. What are sentence-completion tests? Should teachers use them? If so, under what restrictions and circumstances?
8. If a teacher feels that parents are in some way impeding the educational progress of their child, does the teacher have an obligation to rectify the situation? Does she have a right to interfere in family affairs? Is it ethical for teachers to get information from students about their home life?
9. Assume that Miss Purcell's hypothesis is correct and that the Baileys do contribute to Tim's excessive compulsivity for high grades. In what ways could they act differently at home to reduce Tim's problems?
10. How should Miss Purcell handle the conference? How can she get Tim's parents to examine their relationship with Tim without their becoming threatened and defensive? What effect does threatening information have on learning? In general, what can a teacher do to increase the chances for a successful teacher-parent conference?

On the fringe

It is the end of the lunch break in a small, rural elementary school. Most of the students have finished lunch and are playing during the few remaining moments before the bell rings. A group of fifth-grade students are playing at one end of the playground. Most of the girls are skipping rope or playing hopscotch on a concrete slab which is also being used for basketball practice. Other girls are strolling and talking together; a few are watching the boys play softball.

One 10-year-old boy, John, seems anxious to be chosen next to play on Bruce's team. Johnny is a short, thin, pale child with a shock of sandy hair that keeps falling in his face. He nervously brushes his hair back from his forehead and hops from foot to foot as he tries to get the team leader's attention.

At this moment, Bruce turns around to pick someone to play. Johnny, seemingly unable to contain himself, rushes to Bruce's side.

Johnny: Hey, Bruce, let me play next? Please!
Bruce: (He turns to a larger boy) Okay Bill, you're next.

Johnny goes back to the sidelines and continues to fidget and jump up and down. He shouts encouragement to the players on Bruce's team and yells excitedly when the team scores.

Bruce turns to pick another player, sees Johnny waiting tensely to see if he will be picked, and motions him forward with a shrug.

Bruce: Okay John, now get in there.

Johnny: Watch me!

He stops long enough to borrow a glove from one of the other boys, then runs onto the playing field. Johnny runs with an awkward gait and a distinct shuffle in his movements. He appears poorly coordinated. He misses an easy catch and the children on the sidelines call out their dissatisfaction as the batter reaches first base.

One student: Aw, Bruce, what did you let him play for anyway?

Another student: Johnny can't play. Take him out.

Another student: Butterfingers!

Johnny is involved in only the one play before the bell rings and the children slowly pile their softball equipment on a bench and troop back into class. Several students talk to themselves as they walk off the playground.

One student: We always have to quit—just when we're going good.

Johnny: (As he runs to Bruce) I wouldn't have missed if Larry's glove wasn't so big. (He adds, pleadingly) Will you give me another chance, Bruce?

Bruce: (Nodding casually) Yeah, maybe. If the glove's too big, why don't you bring your own sometime instead of mooching off the other kids all the time.

Johnny: (With a sheepish smile) Uh, well, okay. But, will you let me play outfield again?

Bruce: (Over his shoulder as he runs into the classroom) Maybe.

Johnny, walking with a dejected air, is the last to enter the classroom as the final bell rings. Mrs. Lynch, the teacher, is writing an arithmetic assignment on the board as Johnny goes to his seat.

The classroom which Johnny enters is a large room with faded green walls. The walls are covered with the students' art work, and there is a reading center in the back of the room. The desks are old, with tops that open. They are arranged in neat rows, facing the teacher's desk. Johnny takes his seat at the last desk in the row next to the window. He slowly opens the top of his desk to get a pencil and paper.

Johnny: (To himself) Maybe if I practice at home some, I can get to be a really good ballplayer like Bruce someday.

Johnny remains motionless for a long minute, his arm still supporting the hinged top of his desk. He is aroused from his dream when the teacher turns and faces the class. Mrs. Lynch is a middle-aged woman of average size. She has a sweet, unlined faced and a gentle but firm manner.

Mrs. Lynch: Class, this is your assignment for tomorrow. Take time now to jot it down in your notebook so you won't forget it. (She pauses as the students copy down the assignment) Now, I want all of you to get out your homework that you did last night so that we can go over it in class. (She nods toward Johnny) Johnny, you take problem number 1 and put it on the board; Ruth, you take number 2; Annie, number 3; Bruce, number 4; and Mark, number 5. The rest of the class please check your problems at your seats.

Johnny, slowly shuffling through some papers at his desk, is the last to go to the board. On the way to the board he stops by another child's desk.

Johnny: (Tugging at Kirk's sleeve) Hey, help me out, will you? I don't have my paper. Slip me your paper quick!

Mrs. Lynch: (Seeing the exchange) Johnny, do you have your work? (She crosses to him)

Johnny: (In an almost inaudible tone) No . . . no. I can't do these problems.

Mrs. Lynch: (Sighing) How many times does that make this week? (Johnny stands looking down at his feet) I just don't understand you, Johnny. You don't even try. You can do these problems. They're easy. And your brother David was such a good student! I never knew him not to do *his* homework—not once. (Johnny shifts position and looks uncomfortable as the other children laugh softly) Can you work the problem at the board even though you didn't do the homework last night? (Johnny nods his head negatively) Then, (Firmly) go back to your seat, Johnny.

Mrs. Lynch looks around the room and frowns. All laughter ceases. She motions to Kirk.

Mrs. Lynch: Kirk, will you take problem 1 since Johnny can't do it.

The other children exchange smiles and lift their eyebrows as Johnny goes back to his desk and Kirk goes to the board. After Kirk hastily puts the problem on the board, Mrs. Lynch motions all the children at the board back to their seats.

Mrs. Lynch: All right, children, let's check the work at the board. First, let's check Kirk's work. Is it correct?

Mary: (Raising her hand) Kirk put the decimal in the wrong place, Mrs. Lynch.

Johnny gives a loud snort of derision at Kirk's mistake and claps his hands together as Mrs. Lynch turns and gives him a long, hard look of exasperation.

A few weeks later. Mrs. Lynch, pointer in hand, is at the blackboard discussing an arithmetic problem.

Mrs. Lynch: And so, you see, class, it's simply a matter of paying close attention to what you are doing. (Looking at Johnny) You can all do these problems. Many of you make mistakes out of carelessness. Now, all of you try the next five problems by yourself. Raise your hand if you run into any difficulty, and I'll stop by your desk and we'll work it out together.

Johnny, along with the other children, begins to work. After a few minutes Johnny scratches vigorously through the problem on which he is working and breaks the lead point of his pencil. He leans to his right and touches Mary's arm in an attempt to borrow a pencil from her, but she ignores him. He looks around, examines the point of his pencil, and walks to the pencil sharpener. En route he stops and punches Kirk in the arm. Kirk trips Johnny who stumbles and almost falls. He turns and gives Kirk a sharp jab on the shoulder. Kirk makes a lunge at Johnny and the two of them become immediately involved in a vigorous fight.

Mrs. Lynch: (Turning toward the disturbance) Boys! Boys! Stop that immediately. (She moves to separate them and gently shoves Johnny back to his seat)

Johnny: (Protesting, over his shoulder) Mrs. Lynch, Kirk was bothering me. I was just on my way to the pencil sharpener and. . . .

Kirk: (Interrupting) He hit me! He hit me and I hit him back.

Mary: I saw it, teacher. Johnny hit Kirk as he walked by his desk. (Johnny turns and gives Mary a look of disgust)

Mrs. Lynch: All right, that's enough from all of you. Johnny, you know better than to disrupt class. Since you can't use class study time very effectively, I think you need a little extra study time after school.

Johnny: (Protesting vigorously) But, but . . . Bruce said he would let me borrow his glove today and we could practice ball after school.

Mrs. Lynch: I'm sorry, young man. You should have thought of that sooner.

Johnny: (Under his breath) Aw, no! I knew something would happen! (He returns to his seat) Bruce will never help me again! (He bends over his book and brushes at a tear that is forming in his eye)

Later that afternoon, the last bell rings and the children begin to collect their books and coats and leave the classroom. Johnny remains behind with a downcast look on his face. One of the other children stops to talk to the teacher at the door. Johnny goes to the window. He sees Bruce and a few other boys practicing ball on the school playground. Johnny goes dejectedly to his desk and sits moping with his head supported by his left hand. With his right hand he punches holes in the pages of his arithmetic book with a pencil. Mrs. Lynch finishes the conversation with the other child, turns, and sees what Johnny is doing.

Mrs. Lynch: (Walking quickly to Johnny's desk) Johnny, what in the world are you doing? (She takes the book forcefully from him) Here I keep you after school to work on your arithmetic, and you end up ruining the pages of the book. (Johnny sits mutely, biting the eraser of his pencil) Don't you have any respect for other people's property? (She stands a long minute over Johnny, who keep his eyes lowered)

Mrs. Lynch: Johnny, I ought to send you to the principal for mutilating this book. . . . (She stops short at the sight of Johnny's pained face, then, more gently) But I have a feeling it wouldn't help. Johnny, let's talk a minute. You know, you haven't turned in a homework paper in weeks. Yet, just the other day when I helped you with the written problems in arithmetic you got them all right.

Johnny: But I couldn't have done it if you hadn't helped me.

Mrs. Lynch: Why, Johnny, *you* got the answers. I just told you they were right. (Firmly) Now, why don't you start on the homework for tonight.

Johnny: I'll try, Mrs. Lynch, but I know I can't do it.

Two teachers are seated in the small teachers' lounge as Mrs. Lynch enters. She gets a coke from a machine and then drops into a comfortable, frayed chair.

Mrs. Lynch: (Sighing) What a day!

Mrs. Johnston: (Laughing) Laura, you look as if you've had it!

Mrs. Lynch: Oh, it's nothing big, really . . . just a day of one small frustration after another. (She sighs again) Sometimes I think I can handle the big problems better than I can all these pesky little ones. Take today, for example. I've got one child I just can't reach—Johnny Miller. He's quiet in a way. . . . (She sighs) But he doesn't pay attention . . . won't sit still for more than a few minutes at a time. Today during study period I casually looked up from my desk and saw him completely across the room from his desk, picking on another child who was trying to study. And then, Johnny said with great innocence (She mimics Johnny), "Teacher, Kirk was bothering me!" (The other teachers laugh together in empathy with Mrs. Lynch)

Mrs. Lynch: (Continuing) I think that he honestly believes that he can't do his school work, but he's every bit as smart as his older brother. I even looked his IQ up in his cumulative record to be sure. (She adds) And he's really not a bad child, but I can't get him to study. He likes reading and spelling well enough, but it's impossible to read his writing. Here he is, a fifth grader, and he refuses to capitalize his sentences. And he even uses a small "i" when he writes about himself! (Half to herself) He's so different from David, his brother, who I taught two years ago. Now, David was a wonderful student, in every sense of the word. Bright, friendly, hard working . . . you couldn't help but like him. (She smiles) I was so proud of him when he graduated from elementary school as valedictorian! David was a joy to teach . . . but Johnny!

Mrs. Crouch: I've got Michael, his younger brother, in my first-grade class now. He's such a dear little boy—and bright as a button.

Mrs. Lynch: I may have to retain Johnny this year. How can I pass him on when he doesn't do the work? (She shakes her head) If he just believed in himself a little more. Funny (She pauses), I seem to worry more about Johnny than I do any of the other children, and yet, I have the least success with him. (She smiles, shrugs, and turns to go)

Several weeks later. The last bell rings and the children leave. Mrs.

Lynch remains sitting at her desk grading a few papers. She looks up as a woman enters hurriedly. It is Mrs. Miller, who is about 30, attractive, but appears fatigued and agitated.

Mrs. Lynch: Why, hello, Mrs. Miller. Can I help you?

Mrs. Miller: Oh, Johnny forgot his shoes and socks again. I looked on the playground for them, but they weren't there. I thought they might be here.

Mrs. Lynch walks back to Johnny's desk, looks on the floor around the desk, and then opens the top of his desk.

Mrs. Lynch: I'm afraid they're not here. Do you suppose he left them on the school bus?

Mrs. Miller: (Wearily) Yeah, probably. It's just like that kid! Well, there's another spanking from his dad—that's for sure. (She turns to leave)

Mrs. Lynch: Oh, Mrs. Miller, stay a minute, won't you? While you're here, let's talk a bit about Johnny.

Mrs. Miller: (She sits wearily) That child. (With a sigh) He's been a problem ever since he was a baby. He's a whiner, aggravating, and not a bit like David and Michael. (Pause) I don't know what I'd do without my David. He helps at home as well as any grown person. Even little Michael runs errands—but ask Johnny to help—impossible! You'd have to track him down first. He always sneaks off to watch the older kids play ball.

Mrs. Lynch: Does he ever do any school work at home, Mrs. Miller?

Mrs. Miller: Well, I always tell the children to work after dinner on their lessons. Johnny always says that he can't do his homework.

Mrs. Lynch: Do you or your husband help them with their lessons?

Mrs. Miller: (Somewhat sheepishly) My husband's been so short-tempered lately since he's been laid off. And I'm so tired after working all day at the restaurant that I just go to bed as soon as I get home at 7:00. David, bless his heart, usually fixes the children something to eat and puts them to bed. He tries, I know, but he says he can't get Johnny to do any homework. Johnny keeps whining that he can't do the work, but David says he's just lazy.

Mrs. Lynch: I see. (She pauses) Mrs. Miller, I think I should tell you that Johnny may have to be retained next year. He's just not doing as well as the other children. He has given up on arithmetic, and his other work is suffering, too. He constantly wanders around the classroom instead of doing his work. Frankly, his behavior isn't as good as it could be.

Mrs. Miller: I know. George can spank him every day, but he still keeps lying, losing his good clothes, missing meals, and picking on his little brother. And he never talks to his daddy or me, except in yeses and nos. I hate to say it about my own kid, but sometimes . . . sometimes I think he can't do anything right. (She looks down at her hands, seemingly embarrassed) Well (She pauses), I gotta get back. (She gets up from the chair quickly and walks to the door)

Mrs. Lynch: (Calling after her) Mrs. Miller, stay a minute more. (She goes to her side) I don't really want to fail Johnny. . . .I want to help him if I can.

He's not a bad child, and. . . . (She stops short at the harsh expression on Mrs. Miller's face)

Mrs. Miller: (In a flat tone) Mrs. Lynch, do you really think anybody can do *anything* with that kid? (She turns abruptly and leaves)

A few minutes later, Mrs. Lynch stands at the window watching Mrs. Miller walk across the playground in the shadows of the late afternoon. She stands for a long minute, then turns to her filing cabinet and takes out a folder.

Mrs. Lynch: (She opens the folder and reads aloud quietly to herself) Johnny Miller. First grade—sweet, cooperative, shy child. Second grade —quiet, but eager to learn. Needs to be pushed in most subjects. (Her voice grows stronger) Oh, here it begins, third grade—Johnny won't cooperate; doesn't seem to have an interest in school. Doesn't do his homework most of the time. (She continues) And fourth grade—slow learner, has no friends, repeatedly must be sent to principal's office for inattention.

Mrs. Lynch pauses, and looks up from the folder. She sits motionless, staring before her with her hands folded. At this moment Mrs. Johnston is seen walking by the door. She stops and enters the classroom where Mrs. Lynch still sits quietly, lost in thought.

Mrs. Johnston: (Calling softly) Laura, you still here too? We're keeping late hours today.

Mrs. Lynch: (Looking up, half startled) Oh, hello, Mary. Come on in and sit a minute.

Mrs. Johnston: (Crossing to Mrs. Lynch's desk) Grading papers? (She glances down and sees the folder in Mrs. Lynch's hands) Oh, Johnny Miller again.

Mrs. Lynch: This poor child—he's not only out of things here at school, he's obviously out of things at home, too. I just had a talk with his mother. She shakes her head in disbelief) It's hard to believe, but both she and her husband seem ready to wash their hands of Johnny—and he's only 10 years old! (She continues, with feeling) And he's not a dull child. The records show that he has an above average IQ, and he can read well above grade level. But everywhere along the way, he's failed. And I'm just about to add still another failure to the ones he's already accumulated. (She looks up, searchingly) What can you do to help a child like this?

CUMULATIVE RECORD

Name:	John Thomas Miller		**Former school:**
Address:	310 South Pine	**Home phone:** 378-7863	**Date entered:** 8-29-64
Father:	William J. Miller	**Occupation:** Bricklayer	**General health:** Good
Mother:	Betty F. Miller	**Occupation:** Waitress	**Handicaps:** None
Siblings:	David J., age 13		**Date of birth:** 9-25-58
	Michael B., age 6		

TEST RECORD

INTELLIGENCE TESTS:

	Form	IQ	Date	Grade
Otis Quick-Scoring	Alpha	112	10-6-65	2
Mental Ability Tests	Beta	109	10-13-67	4

ACADEMIC RECORD

Grades 1-6 (year averages)

	1	2	3	4	5	6
Citizenship	A	A	C	C		
Lang. Arts	B	C	C	C		
Reading	A	B	B	B		
English			C	C		
Spelling	A	B	B	B		
Writing	C	C	C	D		
Social Studies			D	D		
Arithmetic	B	C	D	F		
Music	A	B	B	B		
Science				D		

Grades 7-9 (year averages)

Grades 10-12 (year averages)

COMMENTS: Grade 1: Mrs. Butler, 5-15-65. Sweet, cooperative, shy child.
Grade 2: Mrs. Jones, 5-19-66. Quiet, but eager to learn. Needs to be pushed in most subjects.
Grade 3: Mrs. White, 5-24-67. Johnny won't cooperate; doesn't seem to have an interest in school. Doesn't do his home-work most of the time.
Grade 4: Mrs. Williams, 5-9-68. Slow learner. Has no friends. Repeatedly must be sent to principal's office for inattention.

Questions—"On the fringe"

1. What is the self-concept? How is the self-concept formed? How does the self-concept change?
2. What relationship exists between self-concept and achievement? Between self-concept and motivation? Between self-concept and learning? What should the teacher do in the classroom to take into consideration these relationships?
3. How does Johnny see himself? How would he like to be different? How have Johnny's siblings contributed to his self-perceptions? Do the perceptions about Johnny held by his parents and siblings agree with Johnny's perceptions of self?
4. In what ways has the school played a role in Johnny's perceptions of self? What influences have the teachers and those in authority had? How have his relationships with his peers helped shape his perceptions of self?
5. How important is social acceptability in children Johnny's age? What experiences could Mrs. Lynch provide for Johnny in interactions with other children? What else should Mrs. Lynch do to help Johnny?

The disinterested one

Westwood Elementary School is located in a middle-class suburb of a large midwestern city. Community support for the school and school system is strong in the form of large PTA attendance and tax support. Every bond issue and tax referendum proposed has passed by a substantial majority.

The school yard is well kept, but the building itself has the austerity associated with the architecture of the 1920s. A few last stragglers climb up the steps to the school before the final bell. A shiny station wagon driven by a maid pulls up in front of the school and an 11-year-old boy of shorter-than-average height gets out.

Maid: Hurry, Jimmy, or you'll be late again!

Jimmy Jackson doesn't answer, but slowly walks to the steps of the school as the station wagon drives away.

Jimmy enters Mr. Smith's sixth-grade classroom late and takes his seat. The classroom is smaller than the usual sized self-contained classroom. It has only one blackboard and one bulletin board. The 31 desks are set in regimented lines facing the front of the room. Some of the children are talking and milling around although the final bell has already rung. Mr. Smith, who is in his fifth year of teaching, calls the class to attention. The children quiet down and take their seats.

Mr. Smith: (Pleasantly) As you know, each morning we have a time for all to share experiences with each other. (Looks at Jim) Jim, you promised to bring your airplane and space collection to school today.

Jim: (Shrugs) I forgot.

Mr. Smith: Will you bring it tomorrow?

Jim: I'll try.

Mr. Smith: All right then. (Calling on another student) Susan, you have your hand up.

It is the next day. Jim is standing in front of the room holding an airplane. On the teacher's desk are various other airplanes and a few books on space ships.

Mr. Smith: Jim, I understand you are very interested in airplanes and the future of space travel. Will you tell us about it?

Jim: (Reluctantly) There isn't much to tell.

Mr. Smith: I'm sure we would be very interested in hearing what you do have to share. (He motions for him to begin)

Jim: Well, this is a B–52 bomber; this is a DC–3; this is a Lear Jet; this is a Boeing 707; and this is a Boeing 727. I have a model of the Apollo rocket which has a space capsule on top. I was interested in these, but I'm kind of tired of them now.

Later that day, the students are working on a social science report. Some are talking together, but all are seated except Jim who is wandering around the room. Mr. Smith calls Jim to his desk.

Mr. Smith: (Kindly) Jim, why do you persist in wandering around the room when you are supposed to be in your seat?

Jim: (Shrugging) I don't know.

Mr. Smith: Have you finished your assignment?

Jim: No.

Mr. Smith: Then, why do you spend so much time away from your desk?

Jim: 'Cause I couldn't think.

Mr. Smith: Does moving around the classroom help you to think?

Jim: (Quietly) Sometimes.

Mr. Smith: Doesn't it bother you when you don't finish your assignments?

Jim: I finish as much as I can.

It is later the same day in the faculty lounge. Teachers are sitting and drinking coffee; some are looking at papers. Mr. Smith enters, goes over to another male teacher, and starts talking.

Mr. Smith: Bob, you had Jim Jackson in the fourth grade. Did you have trouble getting him interested in his work?

Bob: He was pretty hard to reach, but he doesn't have to worry—his old man will take care of him.

Teacher I: I had Jim in the first grade. I didn't dare fail him. His parents would have caused all kinds of trouble.

Teacher II: I have Jim in music and if it weren't for his participation in singing, I would have to fail him.

Bob: Maybe you should have a conference with his parents, if you can get them to come to school. I tried to talk to them when I had Jim, but his old man is too busy with business, and his mother has her volunteer activities at the hospital.

Several days later, Mr. Smith's classroom is empty except for Mr. Smith and Jim's mother. Mrs. Jackson is talking intently.

Mrs. Jackson: I don't know what we can do with Jimmy; we had such good plans for him. His father has already set aside an ample amount of money for his college education. We hope he will snap out of this problem so that he can go to Princeton where his father went.

Mr. Smith: Do you think that you could set aside a definite time to be with Jimmy during the evening to review his work or just talk?

Mrs. Jackson: I'd love to do that, but I have definite commitments at the hospital that I must keep. (She pauses) And anyway—we provide Jimmy with everything he wants. He has a beautiful room, and our Nancy caters to his every wish. We have a country club membership so he can use the pool, play golf, and associate with lots of nice children. (With vigor) And that's another thing—his father is a little concerned about his leadership with other children. They seem to take over when they come to our house to play. Isn't there any way that you can help him become a leader at school?

It is the next day in class. Jim hands Mr. Smith a completed homework assignment.

Mr. Smith: Jim, is this the best work that you can do?

Jim: (Shrugs) I guess so.

Mr. Smith: Are you sure?

Jim, with downcast eyes, shrugs and remains silent. Mr. Smith waits for an answer, but there is none.

At the end of the same day, the children are handing in papers. Mr. Smith counts them and looks at Jim.

Mr. Smith: Jim, do you have your homework assignment completed?

Jim: I didn't know we had to turn it in today.

Mr. Smith: Then you will have to stay after school again to work on it. (To himself) I guess I had better make a home visit and try to talk to both parents.

Mr. Smith sits in a plush livingroom with Mr. and Mrs. Jackson. They are talking.

Mr. Jackson: I hope you will be able to do something for Jim—we have been a little unhappy for some time now with Jim's performance in school. He's been quite a disappointment to me after all I've done for him and promised him. The men at the office say that I should send him to a private military academy, and I may do that.

Mr. Smith: I would like to help Jim, but I will need you to help me. Do you think you could spend a little time each evening with Jim; maybe just talking to him about what he did during the day or reviewing his work in school?

Mr. Jackson: (Shaking his head) I'm a busy man. I've had to work my way to the top and I know what it takes to get there. Once you make it, it's not so easy to stay there—takes a lot of time.

Mr. Smith: I see. Well, how does Jim use his time at home? Many times he has to stay after school to finish a homework assignment.

Mrs. Jackson: He spends most of his time in his room. (With pride) Would you like to see it?

Mr. Smith follows Mr. Jackson to Jimmy's spacious room. It is neatly arranged and well equipped for study or play. Jim's major interests seem to be airplanes and space craft as evidenced by the neatly constructed models.

Mr. Smith: Mr. Jackson, do you help Jimmy with these models? They are really well constructed!

Mr. Jackson: No, I wish I could find more time to do this sort of thing with my son, but the pressures of business limit my time at home. You know how it is. . . .

The next day in the principal's office, Mr. Smith and a guidance counselor are sitting in front of the principal's desk. The principal, Mr. King, sits on a swivel chair behind the desk.

Mr. King: Well, I see by his cumulative record that he is not dumb according to IQ tests he has taken. But I also see that he has made mostly C's and D's in his academic subjects and B's in art and physical education.

Guidance Counselor: He's never been a discipline problem and when we have talked, he answers my questions—although he seems a little withdrawn. He seems to come from an environment that offers him every advantage. He certainly couldn't be called deprived by any stretch of the imagination.

Mr. Smith: (Shaking his head) But in spite of all that he still seems to lose interest. (With concern) What can I do?

CUMULATIVE RECORD

Westwood Elementary School

Name:	Jackson, James J., Jr.
Address:	43 Park Lane Drive
Father:	Jackson, James J.
Mother:	Jackson, Vera
Siblings:	None

Home phone:	644-8323
Occupation:	Vice-pres., Peoples Savings
Occupation:	Housewife

Former school:	
Date entered:	8-29-64
General health:	Excellent
Handicaps:	None
Date of birth:	8-20-58
Age:	11

TEST RECORD

INTELLIGENCE TESTS:

California Test of Mental Maturity:

	CA	MA	IQ	Date	Grade
Language	8-9	9-2	105	5-21-67	3
Non-language	8-9	8-10	101		
		9-0	103		
Stanford-Binet		11-6	115	9-10-68	5

ACADEMIC RECORD

Record the year's average as A, B, C, D, or F:

	Grade 1	Grade 2	Grade 3	Grade 4	Grade 5	Grade 6*
Reading	C	C	C	C	C	C
English			C	C	C	C
Writing	D	D	C	D	C	D
Spelling	C	C	C	D	D	D
Arithmetic	C	C	C	C	C	D
Social Studies			D	C	D	C
Science and Health			C	C	D	C
Art	B	B	B	C	B	B
Physical Education	B		C	B	B	B
Industrial Arts					B	B
Music			B	B	B	C

Write *Below, Average,* or *Above* to indicate level of accomplishment:

WORK HABITS	Average	Average	Below	Below	Below	Below
SOC. AND PERSONAL DEVELOPMENT	Average	Below	Below	Below	Below	Below

* This is only the first six weeks' averages.

Questions—"The disinterested one"

1. Why is Jim disinterested in his school work?
2. How has Jim's home life contributed to his disinterest?
3. Is Jim deprived in any way?
4. How has the school contributed to his disinterest?
5. What is motivation and how is it related to interests and needs?
6. What are Jim's interests and needs?
7. Looking at the world through Jim's eyes, how does he probably perceive his parents? His home life? His classroom? His teacher? His school work?
8. How does Jim probably see himself?
9. Is human motivation something that is internal or external to the individual?
10. What relationships exist between motivation and learning?
11. Is there anything that Mr. Smith can do to help motivate Jim?

Making do

Bryant Elementary School is located in a southern city with a population of over 100,000. Mary Ann Williams is 21 years old and is just beginning her career as a fifth-grade teacher. A large percentage of the pupils in the school are black, and the majority of the parents are low income and highly transient.

As Mary Ann parks her car in the school's dirt parking lot, she looks up at the square-shaped, faded red brick, two-story school building surrounded by a lawn that hasn't been mowed for some time. Paper, candy bar wrappers, and other debris clutter the lawn. The neighborhood surrounding the school is low income, and Mary Ann notices that an automobile repair shop borders the dirt playground which is surrounded by a metal fence. She looks at the cornerstone of the school which says "Erected 1908."

In getting out of her car, Mary Ann speaks to the middle-aged woman who has just gotten out of the car next to hers.

Mary Ann: Hi! I'm Mary Ann Williams. I'm a brand new fifth-grade teacher!

Jane: (Smiling) Glad to know you, Mary Ann. I'm Jane Carson. I teach third grade and I'm definitely not brand new. (Mary Ann and Jane both laugh) Come on and I'll walk you to the teachers' meeting. How did you get stuck at Bryant? (They walk toward the building together)

Mary Ann: Stuck? Is it that bad? I noticed that the building looked old. This is the first time that I have seen it. I was hired downtown and didn't get a chance to visit Bryant. In fact, I wasn't really sure what school I was going to teach in at the time the Superintendent hired me.

Jane: I'll bet you never make that mistake again. Bryant is one of the worst schools in the city.

Mary Ann: (Suspiciously) What's wrong with it?

Jane: Well, not only is the building in bad shape but the facilities are terrible. I think that you'll find that you won't have any supplies in your room.

Mary Ann: Really!

Jane: Really. Oh, yeah—don't count on getting any help with students who need remedial work. Believe me, there'll be a lot of those.

Mary Ann: (Raises her eyebrows) Wow! It sounds like it's going to be a great year! (Mary Ann and Jane enter the building talking)

Mary Ann, Jane, 17 other female teachers of varying ages, and 2 male teachers in their early 20s are seated in the school library for the first teachers' meeting of the year. As the principal, John Cameron, finishes introducing 14 new teachers, Mary Ann looks about the room. The furniture in the room is old and the books take up only about half the available shelf space. Some plaster hangs down from the ceiling over the librarian's desk. The walls and ceilings at Bryant are all painted dark green.

Mary Ann leans over and whispers with a new teacher, Sally, who is seated next to her.

Sally: Have you been to your room yet? (Mary Ann nods her head negatively) I've got news for you—you won't have many books in there either. None of the rooms do.

Mary Ann: (Whispers louder and frowns) Oh, brother!

An experienced teacher, Nancy, who has listened to their conversation, turns around in a seat in front of them, smiles, and speaks in a low voice.

Nancy: Just wait until this winter, girls, when the heating goes out. You can depend on it.

Mary Ann looks at Sally and shakes her head gravely. Both turn their attention to Mr. Cameron who is standing in front of the librarian's desk.

Mr. Cameron: I know that you new people have heard about some of Bryant's shortcomings. Our building is old and we have limited facilities, teaching materials, and auxiliary services. The school board wants to build a new school in this district and doesn't want to keep putting money into a building that is eventually going to be torn down. Our problem is that some citizens have opposed building the new school and have held up its construction with court injunctions for five years now. (He moves to another position in front of the desk and continues) What the board has done, however, is place the most competent staff available in this school—you people. You are a real elite group of teachers and I want you to know that I am proud to work with you. Only a group of top-flight professionals like yourselves could use your imagination and creativity and make do with what equipment we have. If I can be of assistance in any way, please let me know. (Mr. Cameron pauses and looks down at a clipboard) Now for your room assignments. Mrs. Williams, you'll be in Room 211.

Mary Ann enters her classroom. The walls are green, the bulletin board is bare, and the floors have not been waxed for years. Large pictures of Washington and Lincoln are the only pictures on the faded dark green walls. The furniture is blond, movable, and fairly new. A couple of empty animal cages, part of a rock collection, and an old box of flashcards sit on a table in the back of the room. As Mary Ann begins to unload supplies from a cardboard box that she has set on top of her desk, the custodian passes by the door with a broom and shovel. Mary Ann turns toward the door and speaks to him.

Mary Ann: Pardon me, but are you the custodian?
Custodian: Yes, Ma'am, I am.
Mary Ann: I'm Mary Ann Williams. I'll be teaching fifth grade in this room.
Custodian: Glad to meet you, Mrs. Williams. I'm George Rhea.
Mary Ann: Mr. Rhea, I noticed that there isn't any chalk or erasers in the room.
Custodian: I'll pass them out first thing in the morning. I can only give you two erasers and a half dozen pieces of chalk though. We have to ration them.
Mary Ann: (Frowning and raising her voice) Are you kidding? Surely you can do better than that!
Custodian: No, Ma'am. I'm sorry. You'll have to talk to Mr. Cameron if you need more.
Mary Ann: (Firmly) You can bet that I'm going to talk to Mr. Cameron. This is ridiculous!

Mary Ann and Mr. Cameron are seated in his office.

Mr. Cameron: I'm sorry, Mary Ann, but if I didn't ration the chalk and the duplicating paper, we'd simply run out. What's more, we don't even have funds for new books, and I know that you need them badly.
Mary Ann: Mr. Cameron, this is unbelievable. I don't see how the board can expect anyone to teach under these conditions!
Mr. Cameron: Mary Ann, I am on the Superintendent's back every other day. He knows that we have problems here and keeps the board informed. (Stands up) Let me work on it and see what I can do to get you some more equipment for your room.
Mary Ann: (Stands up and smiles) Thank you, Mr. Cameron. Until then I guess I'll just have to make do with what I have.

It is the beginning of the first day of classes and Mary Ann talks to the experienced teacher, Suzie Arnold, who teaches fourth grade in the room next door. They stand in front of the door to Suzie's room as they wait for the children to arrive.

Suzie: There isn't any indoor play area for physical education at all, and have you visited the rest rooms yet?

Mary Ann: No.

Suzie: Just wait. You won't believe it! The acoustics in these classrooms are unbelievably bad. (Looks into her classroom and points toward the ceiling)

Mary Ann: What's wrong with the rest rooms?

Suzie: (Leans back against the door to her room) Half the time the plumbing doesn't work and the toilets—well, they're just worn out.

Mary Ann: Why do the parents put up with this? Can't the parent-faculty organization do anything?

Suzie: (With resignation) The parents just don't seem to care. The PFO held two meetings last year. By the second meeting only teachers were attending. It's been that way for several years.

Mary Ann: What about Mr. Cameron—can't he do anything?

Suzie: (Frowning) I think you'll find that Mr. Cameron is a yes-man for the Superintendent—both of them are yes-men for the board.

Mary Ann: Has anyone taken this to the ATO?

Suzie: (Frowning) A group of us went to the state American Teachers Organization executive committee when they made some of us teach in rooms in the basement that they converted into classrooms. (Raises her voice) We like to froze to death when the heat went out as usual in the winter! (Shifts her weight from one foot to another) They promised to investigate the situation so Cameron moved me up here (Points to her classroom) and put a new teacher in my old room. (Shakes her head with resignation) Forget about the local ATO—it's just plain defunct.

Mary Ann: Do they really plan to build a new building?

Suzie: Who knows? They've been saying that for five years now. As cheap as the school board is I sometimes wonder if they haven't deliberately encouraged some of those injunctions. (Listens to the sound of children's voices and looks down the stairs) Oh, oh! Here they come—the youth of America!

Mary Ann sits in Mr. Cameron's office with the door closed.

Mary Ann: After four weeks I've discovered that five of my children have a four-to-ten-word reading vocabulary and some of the others aren't much better off. They need remedial help. Thirty-four children is a big load to begin with, but when you. . . . (She is interrupted by Mr. Cameron)

Mr. Cameron: I'm sorry, Mary Ann, but remedial help isn't available in this school system until the seventh grade. Put your problem readers in a group by themselves and budget your time carefully so that you can spend as much time as possible with them. (Smiles, then stands up. Mary Ann then stands up) I'll tell you what—I usually have a free hour around 11 o'clock. I'll come in from time to time and work with them myself. (Moves over to Mary Ann, puts his hand on her shoulder and gently guides her to the door) I know that your job is difficult and all I ask of you is that you do the very best that you can under the circumstances. I know that you'll do your best because you're a pro!

Mary Ann sits at home in the livingroom of her comfortable middle-class home with her husband, Jerry, an electrical engineer, who is reading the evening paper and at the same listening to Mary Ann talk.

Mary Ann: Jerry, I know that you get tired of hearing me talk about it but I get tired of batting my head against a stone wall every day.

Jerry: (With resignation) Do we have to go through that again! (The telephone rings) You'd better get the phone. (Mary Ann walks into the kitchen and picks up the phone)

Mary Ann: Hello—Williams residence.

Voice: Is this Mary Ann Williams?

Mary Ann: (Cautiously) Yes, it is. Who is this?

Voice: Mary Ann, this is George Sanders, the Superintendent. I wanted to call you to let you know that I appreciate the effort that you are making at Bryant. Mr. Cameron has been telling me about the fine job you have been doing and the handicaps under which you and the other teachers at Bryant have been working. I also want you to know that the board and I are doing all we can to get the new building underway.

Mary Ann: (In a surprised and pleased manner) Thank you very much, Mr. Sanders. I do the best that I can under the circumstances.

Mr. Sanders: I know that, Mary Ann, and want you to know that I appreciate it. Our school system isn't a wealthy one since our tax base is primarily low income. But sooner or later we'll get the job done. In the meantime, I want to thank you for being a pro and making do with what little you have to work with.

Mary Ann: Thank you so much, Mr. Sanders! I know that your job is a difficult one. I really appreciate your taking the time to call me.

Mr. Sanders: If I can help you at any time, just let me know. I've enjoyed talking to you.

Mary Ann: Thanks again.

Mr. Sanders: Goodbye.

Mary Ann: Goodbye. (Mary Ann hangs up the phone slowly and stares out into space, she then walks slowly back into the living room) Jerry, do you know who that was?

Jerry: No. Who?

Mary Ann: Sanders—the Superintendent. He called me to thank me for being a good teacher.

Jerry: (With a smirk on his face) He did, huh? So how do you feel about that?

Mary Ann: I don't know how I feel—I have mixed emotions. What do you think?

Jerry: Do you really want to know?

Mary Ann: Yes. Tell me.

Jerry: Well, I think that a pat on the back is a poor substitute for decent teaching conditions, but it looks like it has worked at Bryant for some time.

Mary Ann: Jerry, do you think that I should go talk to Mr. Sanders and ask him to transfer me to another school?

Questions—"Making do"

1. What is a professional? To what extent is the teacher a professional? How do Mr. Cameron and Mr. Sanders seem to define the term?
2. What is learning? Does it differ from achievement? Do conditions like the ones described at Bryant actually affect learning?
3. What does Suzie mean when she describes Mr. Cameron and Mr. Sanders as yes-men? What is power and who holds power in a school system? How much power do Mr. Cameron and Mr. Sanders seem to have and how has it affected their behavior? Would it be desirable for the ATO to have more power?
4. To what extent are the parents of Bryant responsible for the school's condition? What values do they seem to possess toward education? How do such values develop? How do such values change?
5. Are auxiliary services such as remedial reading really necessary at the elementary level? What auxiliary services do you feel are essential?
6. Do teachers as a professional group seem to have a common set of needs that motivate their behavior? What is frustration and how does it affect teacher behavior? What is teacher morale? To what extent do variables outside the classroom affect what goes on inside?
7. What value are parent-teacher organizations? Could a strong PFO really help the situation at Bryant? How does a strong PFO develop?
8. When a teacher finds herself in a situation like Mary Ann, should she try to be cooperative and do the very best that she can under the circumstances or will it only be solving the school board and school administration's problems for them?
9. What should Mary Ann do? Should she resign now or at the end of the year? Should she ask the Superintendent to transfer her to another school? Should she try to stay at Bryant and work for change? If so, how should she go about working for change?

Mary, Mary, quite contrary

John Cook is a black, eighth-grade math teacher with five years' teaching experience. He teaches in an old but well-kept school located in a city of 100,000 in a southeastern state. The school serves both black (20 percent of student body) and white children and draws pupils from both low-income (60 percent) and middle-income families.

A bell rings. Scuffling, a concerto of voices, and other noises are heard in the background. In Mr. Cooks' classroom, there are several graphs and charts on the wall. An overhead projector sits in one corner. There is a poster at the front of the room with the commutative, associative, and distributive properties displayed. There is also a chart of common fractions and decimal equivalents. Several geometric models are on the desk. Mr. Cook is standing by a desk putting some papers in order. The footsteps and voices of the students get louder as they file into the room. Most go immediately to their seats. The tardy bell rings. One student sharpening his pencil rushes to sit down. Voices are reduced to a whisper, with an occasional comment rising above the hum. Mr. Cook looks up and scans the seats. One is conspicuously empty. He runs his finger down the page and then across.

Mr. Cook: (To himself) The only time Mary has ever been absent was when she was suspended. (He turns to the class) Mary appears to be absent today?

Tom: She was sure here last period. Was that something. . . . She beat up Carol and when Mrs. Snyder pulled them apart, Mary was so mad she rammed her head through the window. You should have seen Mrs. Snyder!

The class comes alive. All eyes are focused on Tom. Each student clamors to question him about the details. (Said almost in unison)
Student: I'll bet Snyder had a fit. What'd she do?
Another student: What did old Thomas do?
Another student: Is Carol hurt? That must have been something when Mary broke the window!
Tom: You better believe it was something. Mrs. Snyder. . . .

The door bangs open. In rushes a large, well-developed 15-year-old white girl, taller than any of the girls and many of the boys in the class. Her plain green dress is in disarray. She has only sandals on her feet. Her face is flushed. She walks over to Mr. Cook, and hands him a piece of paper.
Mary: (Blatantly) I just beat the hell out of Carol, and almost got suspended. (Without pausing) She was telling some kids some things about me.

The class reaction is pandemonium. Students move about restlessly in their seats. Voices are loud . . . some trying to question Mary, others talking about it among themselves. Mary is talking loudly to no one in particular. In the din it is difficult to distinguish what is being said. Mr. Cook, anxious to restore order, bangs on his desk with his hand.

Mr. Cook: (Loudly) Class!

The somewhat startled class calms down, although there is still a faint murmur of voices. The air is one of general excitement. Mary also is quiet, but she is staring at Mr. Cook, almost as if she is defying him to take action.

Mr. Cook: (Reads note to himself) "Mary disrupted Mrs. Snyder's English class again. She had a disagreement with Carol Lee in the classroom and it ended with Mary breaking one of the classroom windows. I have talked with her, and she understands that if she is back in the office again this week she will be suspended for three days. If her conduct isn't what it should be, send her back to me at once. Mr. Thomas." (He glances up and nods toward Mary) Mary, why don't you take your seat, and I'll continue checking the roll. (Turns to the class) Class, let's get quiet, please!

The class, however, is still anxious to hear more about Mary's fight. The students are talking among themselves, and some are tossing taunting remarks at Mary who is visibly distraught.

Mary: (Standing at the front of the room, arms waving wildly) Shut up, shut up, or I'll throw you out. We've got to take the roll. (She reaches out to strike at Tom, who had been loudest in his teasing)
Mr. Cook: (Firmly) Mary, you take care of yourself, and I'll take care of the class. Go to your seat.
Mary: (Turns toward Mr. Cook, her face contorted with anger) I hate teachers . . . niggers most of all.

Mr. Cook: (With restraint) Mary, return to the principal's office. Now, this minute!

Mary turns to go, looks up reflectively. Her mouth opens as if to say something, but she says nothing. She walks out, letting the door slam behind her.

Mr. Cook sits in the guidance office looking over Mary's cumulative folder. Mrs. Scott, the school guidance counselor, enters while Mr. Cook is looking at Mary's record.

Mrs. Scott: Good afternoon, Mr. Cook. Who are you looking up?

Mr. Cook: (With a sigh) The school's biggest problem—Mary Ann Johnson.

Mrs. Scott: Yes, I heard she was involved in another fight in Mrs. Snyder's class today. You know, she comes from a very deprived home situation.

Mr. Cook: Yes, I've tried to contact her mother on several occasions. I even went to her house last week, but no one was home. It's difficult to believe anyone lives in that place. It had no window panes, only feed sacks over the windows.

Mrs. Scott: Did you know her Mother was arrested eight days ago on a prostitution charge, and she is still in jail? She has been unable to raise the bond.

Mr. Cook: No, I didn't know. (With interest) Who's taking care of Mary?

Mrs. Scott: There are two older sisters in the home, both in their 20s. Both are unmarried and each has an illegitimate child. There is an older brother but he is presently in the state reformatory on a larceny charge. No one knows where her father is now.

Mr. Cook: (Holding Mary's test record) It appears that she did approximately average work through the fourth grade. Even her achievement test scores in the fifth grade are near grade level. Looking at these grades for the first three grades, one might think she had some ability, but look at this low IQ—87!

Mrs. Scott: Well, I would be inclined to question the validity of that test, since it is the only score we have, and it wasn't given until the sixth grade, when she was already experiencing school difficulties. As a matter of fact, wasn't that the year the family was burned out? (Pointing to the record) Look at the teacher comments.

Mr. Cook: (Reads aloud) In the sixth grade her teacher wrote, "Home burned in November. Stepfather alcoholic and in jail much of the time, but when at home aggressive toward Mary and her two older sisters. Mary doesn't try. Seventh grade—craves attention. Very poor work habits."

Mr. Cook is arranging the books on his desk. He sits down, deep in thought.

Mr. Cook: (To himself) Could I have handled it any differently when I sent Mary out of the room last week? Still, it's annoying when she waves and yells to people out of the window, and that incessant need to run to the pencil sharpener. If I had been Janie, I would have slapped her, too, after that karate chop Mary gave her. What a turmoil that ended in. (He muses for a minute, then continues) Then there was the incident when I sent her to the principal's office for throwing a book when Bill yelled the answer out to the problem she was working on the board. What was it she said —"When I want something from you, I'll knock it out of you." She even demanded that I give her another problem. Back in October she was suspended for three days, but it didn't make any difference in her behavior.

Mr. Cook is in the principal's office. There is a large desk with several chairs around it. Mr. Thomas is sitting at his desk, and Mr. Cook is opposite him. The door to the office is closed.

Mr. Thomas: Yes, I had to suspend her for three days. Perhaps she'll be put in a foster home since I reported the case to the Child Welfare Department. It's really a tragic situation.

Mr. Cook: (Earnestly) Yes, Mr. Thomas, but what are we going to do for Mary when she returns to school?

CUMULATIVE RECORD

Lincoln Junior High School

Name:	Johnson, Mary Ann*	**Former school:**	Wilson Elementary	
Address:	Rt. #3, Box 788B	**Home phone:** None	**Date entered Lincoln:**	
Father:	Johnson, Joe Baker	**Occupation:** Gas Station Attendant	**General health:**	Good
Mother:	Johnson, Jane P.	**Occupation:** Cleaning Woman	**Handicaps:**	None
Siblings:	Joe Franklin, Age 28		**Date of birth:**	1-7-53
	Gloria, Age 25	* Student approved for free lunch.	**Age:**	15
	Anna, Age 22			

TEST RECORD

INTELLIGENCE TESTS:
California Test of Mental Maturity:

	CA	MA	IQ	Date	Grade
Language	12-4	10-3	84	5-14-65	6
Non-language	12-4	11-1	87		

ACHIEVEMENT TEST:
Iowa Test of Basic Skills:

Grade	Lang. Arts Reading	Spelling	English	Math	Science	Social Studies
5	4-1	4-4		5-3	6-0	5-4
6	4-3	4-1	5-1	5-2	6-0	5-8
7	4-5	4-7	5-8	4-9	6-6	6-0

ACADEMIC RECORD

Grade level	1		2		3		4		5		6			Promoted	Retained	Social Promotion
		Promoted		Promoted		Promoted		Promoted		Promoted		Promoted				
Citizenship		2		2		2		3		3		D		D	F
Reading	3	2		5		2		3		4		D		D	D
English		3		3		3		3		3		D		D	D
Spelling	3	3		1		3		3		2		F		F	D
Writing		4		2		3		3		4		D+		C—	
Social Studies		3								4		D		D	D
Arithmetic	3	4		1		3		3		3		F		F	F
Science												C—		C—	

	1	2	Avg.			1	2	Avg.
English	C	D				C	D	D
Social Studies	C	D				C	F	D—
Math	C	F				D	F	D—
Science	D	D				D	D	D
P.E.	F	F				F	F	F
Exploratory							Grade 8	
	Grade 7							

KEY:
(1) Child is working below grade level.
(2) Child is working below grade level, but is making progress.
(3) Child is working at grade level.
(4) Child is doing excellent work at grade level.
(5) Child is working above grade level.

Questions—"Mary, Mary, quite contrary"

1. What is a discipline problem?
2. What is social class and what are the differences between the social classes?
3. To what social class does Mary belong? Why?
4. What values does Mary seem to hold about: (A) physical violence and aggressiveness; (B) sex and dirty language; (C) cleanliness; (D) emotional control; (E) education (F) racial prejudice?
5. What values do Mary's teachers, particularly Mr. Cook, hold about the above topics?
6. What does deprived mean?
7. What role has the home situation played in causing Mary to behave the way that she does in school?
8. How have Mary's peers in school affected her behavior?
9. How does Mary probably see herself? Why?
10. Has Mary's stage of development contributed to her problem?
11. How do you explain the apparent inconsistency between Mary's IQ scores on the one hand and her achievement test scores and grades on the other?
12. Does the school's curriculum seem meaningful to Mary?
13. Why did suspension from school seem to fail to alter Mary's behavior?
14. As Mary turned to leave Mr. Cook's room after being told to go back to the principal's office, she started to say something but didn't. What did she want to say?
15. Assuming that behavior change is desirable in Mary's case, can Mr. Cook and the other school personnel do anything about the forces affecting her behavior?

Mission: impossible

Brown High School is a consolidated, comprehensive high school with grades 7 through 12. It serves the west side of a rural county in a southern state. The school population is approximately 55 percent Negro and 45 percent Caucasian, with a total student body of about 550. The school is brand new; in fact, it is in the process of being completed. Workmen move in and out of classrooms daily, painting and making finishing touches in the carpentry work. Classroom equipment is sparse. Many rooms have an insufficient number of desks. The desks that are available are old and need repair. Most of the desks were originally constructed for use in elementary schools. In many classrooms folding chairs are used in place of desks.

The total effect is one of incongruity. The outside of the school building is modern and attractive. It is shaped like a giant doughnut, with classrooms circled around an atrium. Inside the halls are spacious and carpeted. The brightly painted rooms which open to the halls all appear attractive until the desks and chairs are encountered. The central office is a large, spacious room which houses the principal and his secretary. In one corner large leather chairs and a table provide space for informal conferences. Mailboxes, a key plaque, and filing cabinets line the wall to the right of the entrance. The secretary works in the middle of the room behind a long counter which partially shields the principal's desk.

On this spring morning several teachers are milling around in the office.

Some are talking quietly; a few stand before the bulletin board examining an announcement of coming school events.

Mrs. Towers, a matronly, open-faced woman about 45 years old stands before the mailbox, collecting a sheaf of envelopes and folded papers. She sees a fellow teacher approaching, and her face lights up in a friendly smile. She moves forward a step.

Mrs. Towers: Hi, Mrs. Gates. I've been meaning to chat with you ever since the principal introduced you at the faculty meeting last week. I'm Beth Towers and I teach ninth-grade science. (She extends her hand) Welcome to Brown.

Mrs. Gates is a slim, well-groomed, 31-year-old woman. She graduated from an old southern women's college and did graduate study at a leading privately endowed university. She has two years teaching experience in a private junior high school for girls and eight years teaching experience in a public junior high school located in a middle- and upper middle-class residential area.

Mrs. Gates: (Smiling) Oh, thank you for the welcome. I need it!

Mrs. Towers: How are things going?

Mrs. Gates: Well, (Ruefully) not so well, really. I'm still a little . . . (She hesitates a moment, then continues) a little disoriented, I guess. Somehow, everything seems so unreal.

Mrs. Towers: (Smiling) Yes, I can well imagine. It was hard enough on all of us who moved over here mid-year from our old school. It must have been doubly hard on those of you who were affected by the desegregation ruling. (Pauses in thought) Yes, for those of you who had to change teaching assignments to completely different schools it must have been pretty frustrating.

Mrs. Gates: Oh, it was! (She looks around) There I was, last week in the school where I'd taught for years, where I knew all the children—and their parents, too—(Her voice trails off) everything seemed to run so smoothly there. But here—(She looks around again; this time with a frown on her face) it's all so confused! (With an embarrassed expression on her face she adds, quickly) Oh, I don't mean to imply that this is a *bad* place to be. . . . (Her voice again trails off lamely) It's just . . . different. I'm sure I'll feel right at home soon. (She concludes with bravado)

Mrs. Towers: (With warmth) Yes, I'm sure you will. (She touches Mrs. Gates' arm) Say, why don't you stop by the science lab some afternoon before you go home. We'll go to the lounge, have a coke and talk. I'd like that.

Mrs. Gates: (Smiling) Yes, I'd like that, too! Thank you.

The first bell rings. Mrs. Gates collects her keys from the board of keys and moves to go. In her haste she drops a book which Mrs. Towers retrieves for her.

Mrs. Towers: (Glancing at the title) *The Lives of 10 Great Classical Composers.* . . . Are you going to use this with your music class?

Mrs. Gates: Oh, yes. It's so inspirational. My students loved it at Edgewater. They loved reading about the lives of great composers. So many of the students here seem to need to be exposed to great examples they can follow.

Mrs. Towers: (Hesitantly) Do you really think that these children here will be interested in classical composers?

Mrs. Gates: (Breezily) Sure—they'll love it! You'll see. I've used this material at least six or seven times before and it's always been successful.

Mrs. Gates smiles confidently, gathers her materials, and goes out of the office. She leaves Mrs. Towers standing alone with a slight frown of consternation on her face. Mrs. Towers then shrugs to herself, shakes her head, and turns to go to her first-period science class.

Mrs. Gates walks down the hall to the first-period music class which meets from 8:30 A.M. to 9:15 A.M. daily, Monday through Friday. The class consists of 36 students from the seventh and eighth grades: 11 Caucasian males, 4 Negro males, 5 Caucasian females, and 16 Negro females. Their ages vary from 12 to 15. When Mrs. Gates examined the cumulative records of 5 of the students she found such teacher comments as "undisciplined," "unruly," "aggressive," "loud-mouthed," and "impossible."

Mrs. Gates enters the small classroom which also serves as the music room. The chairs and desks are arranged in a haphazard circle around the teacher's desk. Mrs. Gates places her materials on the desk and proceeds to put a song book on each desk as the last bell rings and the seventh- and eighth-grade children noisily push and shove their way into the room. Desks are moved about, chairs are pulled across the floor, and books are dropped onto the floor. Several students put their other books on top of the music books, or put the music books inside their desks, or take books from the other desks.

Mrs. Gates: (In a moderately firm voice) All right, class, go to your seats. (The talking and the jostling behavior continue)

Mrs. Gates: (Focusing her attention on one child) Rosalyn!

Rosalyn has been standing in the doorway talking to several boys standing in the hall. She turns her head momentarily in Mrs. Gates' direction, ignores the admonition to sit down, and then calmly resumes her discussion. Mrs. Gates appears nonplussed by Rosalyn's behavior and she turns to a child in the back of the room.

Mrs. Gates: Carlos, please sit down. (Carlos is seated in the windowsill)

Carlos: (Mockingly) But I *am* sitting down, teacher!

Mrs. Gates: (With some frustration) Carlos, you know what I mean. (Firmly) In a chair, this minute! (Then, to the rest of the class) Get to your seats!

The noise and the movement in the room continue to mount as the teacher attempts futilely to direct students to their assigned seats. Rosalyn finishes her conversation with the boys in the hallway and slowly takes a seat.

Mrs. Gates: Adam, now I'm going to ask you one more time to move.

Adam makes a face, picks up a chair, puts it noisily into the corner, and stands, shouting at Rosalyn who is laughing at him.

Mrs. Gates: Adam, sit down! (Adam sits, continuing his discourse with Rosalyn across the room)
John: (Yelling across the room to Chester) Hey, Chester! (Chester is watching Rosalyn and Adam; he looks up but does not respond)
Mrs. Gates: Jeanne, will you come over to the seat where you belong?
Jeanne: I don't know where I sit. (Laughter in the class)
John: Sit next to me.

Mrs. Gates walks over to Jeanne's seat and puts her hand on the desk. Jeanne works her way over to the desk, throws her books on the desk, and drops into the seat, smiling. The noise in the room continues. Mrs. Gates goes to the piano.

Mrs. Gates: (Screaming) All right! Whoever continues to talk will be assigned to detention hall! (Pause) Get into the seats you've been assigned to! (Two students come in and slam the door)
Mrs. Gates: (Turning to them) I've told you two for the last time to come in on time. Report to the principal's office, both of you.

The two students leave the room as they came, laughing and talking, slamming the door as they go. There is a new brief period of silence until the fire alarm buzzes (the workmen often set off fire alarms several times weekly). Chester opens the hall door, and the noise from the hall can be heard in the room. Assorted student comments: "Close the door"; "We goin' to catch on fire"; "Make him close the door, Mrs. Gates."

Mrs. Gates: Chester, close the door. (All attention is on Chester)
Chester: (He puts his hand up to his ear and responds) I can't hear you.

The class laughs. Chester finally closes the door and the noise in the room subsides.

Mrs. Gates: We'll start with the school song. Open your music books to page 138.
Several students: We ain't got no books.

At this point there is much searching about for books. Students begin to settle down, with some asking the teacher the page number again; still they are not quiet. Mrs. Gates begins playing the piano, telling the students again the page number in the song book. The class sings the school song, very loudly.

Later, while the class is singing another song, a tapping noise can be heard through the wall. Workmen are still in the process of finishing the gymnasium which is on the other side of this classroom wall. Chester pounds on the wall in response to the tapping.

Tina: Jeanne, your breath smells like raw onions.

Mrs. Gates: Turn to page 161!

Students: We've read that before; we already read that; we done that part.

Mrs. Gates: I'm sorry; turn to page 168.

Students: Do we have to read again today? Why can't we do anything else? (The noise level begins to build up again)

Mrs. Gates: All right, that's enough. (Her voice is strident and the students become quiet; then, in a softer voice she continues) This is a beautiful story about Beethoven's early life as a young musical prodigy. He began composing when he was even younger than you. Now, I want you to take turns reading this essay orally. Jodi, will you begin reading first?

As the children read, they frequently falter and attempt to pronounce words with great difficulty. Most of the students appear diffident about the assignment, and they start shuffling papers on their desks. Carlos begins tapping his pencil on his desk in a distinct rhythm. Rosalyn across the room looks up, winks at Carlos, and begins to accompany him. The beat is contagious and Tina and Joan begin to make bobbing movements with their heads. Finally, the class erupts into hand clapping. Mrs. Gates begins to shout. She turns first to one child, then to another, and then she breaks into sudden tears of frustration. The staccato sounds of the pencil tapping and hand clapping begin to fade away as the students, in a hushed silence, and with expressions of surprise on their faces, sit looking at Mrs. Gates. The bell rings and the children walk in clusters out of the room. A few smile sheepishly but most of them have blank expressions on their faces and do not begin to talk until they enter the hallway.

Mrs. Gates is sitting in the teachers' lounge at the end of the school day. She seems very much alone. Mrs. Towers enters and goes to her side on the couch.

Mrs. Towers: (With concern) Why, what's wrong? You look so dejected!

Mrs. Gates: (In a flood of emotion) Oh, Beth, it's been a perfectly awful day! My first-period class—I can't explain it, but it just fell apart. (She spreads her hands) They just got away from me. (She begins to cry) I've just come from Mr. Rogers (the principal). Somehow, he'd heard all about it. . . . I don't know how or who told him. (She adds, with a grimace) He wasn't very sympathetic. He just kept saying "I know it's a bad situation, but you're a teacher, and I don't want to hear about any more disturbances like this one. (Her voice breaks as she turns to Mrs. Towers) I love children, and I've always thought of myself as a good teacher. (She shakes her head) But I've never had any experience in working with kids like these. They don't seem to be interested in *anything!*

Mrs. Towers: Didn't you tell Mr. Rogers how difficult the children are to handle? I know how they can be.

Mrs. Gates: He said that I'd already sent more students to the office than any other two teachers, and that I'd have to become stricter. He said that I should send the real troublemakers to him, but that I couldn't send the whole class to him. Beth, even if I send the troublemakers to him, the rest of the children just aren't interested in music. Nothing seems to work like it used to. I just don't know what to do. (She stares vacantly into space)

OCCUPATIONAL AND EDUCATIONAL BACKGROUNDS OF THE PARENTS OF FIFTEEN STUDENTS IN MRS. GATES' 8:30 CLASS

Student	Father's occupation	Father's education
1	Purchasing Clerk	Grade 12
2	Machinery Operator	Grade 8
3	Electrician	Grade 5
4	Mechanic	Grade 10
5	Dogcatcher	Grade 6
6	Janitor	Grade 2
7	Egg Loader	Grade 6
8	Truck Driver	Grade 12
9	Logger	Grade 12
10	Truck Driver	Grade 8
11	Truck Driver	Grade 8
12	Orderly in Hospital	Grade 12
13	Egg Loader	Grade 6
14	Laborer	Grade 4
15	Laborer	Grade 4

Questions—"Mission: impossible"

1. What is a discipline problem? Why does Mrs. Gates have a discipline problem? Differentiate between internal and external discipline. How are rewards and punishment related to discipline? What is good discipline? Is it related to learning?
2. What social-class backgrounds seem to be represented in Mrs. Gates' 8:30 class? How do the social classes differ in terms of reward and punishment patterns in the home? From what social class does Mrs. Gates seem to come?
3. What is motivation? How does it relate to discipline and does it vary by social class? Do the students in Mrs. Gates' class seem to be motivated by any of the activities that are taking place? How is motivation related to group dynamics? What group dynamics seem to be operating in this case? What seems to motivate Mrs. Gates? The principal? The class?
4. What is frustration? Are frustration and aggression related? Is there any evidence of frustration in this situation? Do different leadership patterns affect group frustration? How are frustration, motivation, and learning all related? What are the usual consequences of frustration?
5. In what ways has Mrs. Gates contributed to the siituation that has developed? In what ways, if any, should she change her behavior? When she goes into her 8:30 class tomorrow, what should she do? What long-range courses of action should she take? How can she obtain a greater understanding of the situation that confronts her?
6. Is the part of the music curriculum being taught by Mrs. Gates meaningful to the students in her 8:30 class? How can it be made more meaningful? Do you agree with her objective of inspiring the students by providing great examples? What is the best way to attain such an objective? Can teacher-pupil planning be of any assistance here?

The cheaters

The student body of Lincoln Junior High School is gathered in the school auditorium for the orientation assembly at the beginning of the school year. Lincoln is located in a small, middle-class, residential community in the midwest. The principal goes to the podium. After welcoming the new students and introducing some of the faculty members, he starts in on his orientation speech.

Mr. Pierce: Honesty is the best policy. This school has stood for this ideal for 60 years, just as Lincoln himself stood for it 100 years ago. We have never had any serious incidents of dishonesty here at Lincoln Junior High School, and we hope that the new students this year and the old, too, will hold to the responsibility that those before you have held to.

Mrs. Lewis, who is in her third year of teaching, is giving an examination in her American history class. Some of the students grimace as they read the multiple-choice questions. Mrs. Lewis walks up and down the aisle.

Mrs. Lewis: You have three minutes 'til the bell. Please put your papers on my desk as you leave.

Students work on intensely. The bell rings. The students get up and gather their books. They leave the room, after putting the tests on the front desk, grumbling and shaking their heads.

One student to another: Where did she get those questions? She never tests on what she talks about in class!

It is the end of the first grading period. Mrs. Lewis sits at her desk averaging grades in her grade book. Some of the students have very high test grades and very low quiz and homework grades.

Mrs. Lewis: (To herself) This just can't be possible. How could these students be doing so well on tests and so poorly on homework and snap quizzes? (She flips to another class section in the gradebook, comparing the grade differences) In my other sections there are not half as many A's on this test. This one section has too many high grades comparatively. Could they be cheating?

The next day in class, Mrs. Lewis is reviewing the test. She has not handed back the corrected test papers, and is asking the questions orally to quiz each student.

Mrs. Lewis: Who was the governor of New Amsterdam at the time that the British took it over and made it New York? John?
John: Uh . . . I don't know.
Mrs. Lewis: You got it right on the test.
John: I guess I just forgot it.
Mrs. Lewis: Well, Jim. What about this one? Who was the original founder of Georgia?
Jim: James Oglethorpe.
Mrs. Lewis: Fine. And Joey, name the first permanent white settlement in New England and give its founding date. (Silence) Well, Joey?
Joey: Uh-h-h. . . .
Mrs. Lewis: (Firmly) Can't you remember? You had the right answer on your test paper.
Joey: (Nodding) No. (The bell rings and students leave)
Mrs. Lewis: (To herself) That's interesting . . . some of the students who got good grades on their tests can't remember the correct answers now. During the next test I'll just have to watch closely for the passing of answers or cheatsheets.

Three weeks later, Mrs. Lewis is giving another exam. Facial expressions and students' movements are like those at the first test. Mrs. Lewis is proctoring closely. There are no signs of cheating anywhere.

Mrs. Lewis: (To herself) I just can't understand it. How can their grades be so high if they don't cheat? They can't remember the correct answers the very next day!

Some of the students from the American history class are sitting around a booth at a drive-in restaurant. John and Joey are sitting on one side of the table. Another boy, Sam, is seated across from them.

Joey: Brother, old lady Lewis had me sweating in American history today!

John: That was a close call. I can't figure it out. Do you think she was wise to us and didn't give back the papers so she could see if we really knew the answers?

Sam: I answered my question right. That should have thrown her off a little even if she did suspect, and I don't think she did.

Jim, a well-built athlete, enters, walks over to the boys at the table, and sits down.

Jim: Hi! How's it going? Wasn't that history class last period tough? (They nod) I really lucked out on that answer. I only made a C on the test and I studied for three hours. I can't understand it.

John: Yeah, we were having lots of trouble too until we discovered something. Should we tell him?

Joey: Sure.

Sam: Why not? He's good at keeping his mouth shut.

John: Well, it's this way, man. Sam's sister, Linda, had Mrs. Lewis for this class last year. She saved all her tests instead of turning them in at the end of the year because she knew that Sam was going to take it this year.

Joey: It's been an easy ride ever since. Mrs. Lewis hardly changed the tests at all.

John: Do you want to be in with us on it? It's only us and a couple of other guys.

Jim: Well, I don't know; I'll have to think about it. It sounds pretty easy, but I sure wouldn't want to get caught! Well, see you all tomorrow. I'll tell you then. (Jim gets up and leaves; the boys continue talking)

Later that afternoon, Mrs. Lewis is in the main office looking in her mailbox. A fellow teacher enters to look for her mail also.

Mrs. Lewis: Madge, do you have a minute?

Madge: (Nodding) Sure. What is it?

Mrs. Lewis: I think that there has been a group of students cheating in one of my history classes. Do you have any special way you handle such a problem? (Earnestly) I'm really bewildered; this has never happened to me before.

Madge: I just started teaching this year. I've never had to deal with the problem. I won't cross that bridge until I come to it. (She laughs to herself and leaves the office)

Mrs. Lewis: Well, thanks anyhow, Madge. (She looks down at her mail)

She sees a note among the letters which says:

Mrs. Lewis,
Could we see you today in your room about 20 minutes after school is out? It is important. Thank you.

Jim Tanner
Susie George
Mark Snyder

Mrs. Lewis hurries out of the office and down the hall to her classroom. She finds the three students who had signed the note sitting in her classroom. Mrs. Lewis listens to the students tell about the cheating.

Jim: So, Sue, Mark, and I thought it would be best to come to you about it. We all studied hard for that test and only made C's because the curve was set so high. We don't think it's right that those guys should be able to cheat and set the curve.

Susie: It's just ruining our grades and lots of other kids too.

Mark: Isn't there something that you can do, Mrs. Lewis?

Mrs. Lewis: I can start by thanking the three of you for trusting me enough to tell me this. I will see what I can do before tomorrow.

Jim: Well, thanks a lot. We just felt it best to come straight to you. See you tomorrow.

Mrs. Lewis: Okay . . . goodbye.

The next day, near the end of the American history class, Mrs. Lewis finishes her lecture.

Mrs. Lewis: Oh, one more thing before the bell rings. Will John Bunch, Joey Simmons, Sam Krieger, Kent Largo, and Paul Nisner please remain a minute after class. I need to talk to you.

The bell rings. The class gets up, collects their books, and all leave but the five boys. They move up to the desks in front of Mrs. Lewis' desk. Sam is visibly nervous, the others are "keeping cool."

Mrs. Lewis: It has come to my attention, boys, that you are doing very well on your tests and yet you are failing your homework assignments and pop quizzes. I suspected cheating, but not until yesterday did I find out about your using the old tests. Do you have anything to say at this point? (All sit in silence) I really don't know quite what to do. (Pauses, sighs) One thing for sure, I will have to notify your parents. I will probably make up a new set of tests also and give the whole class a retest. Suspension seems in line, but I'll have to talk to the principal about that. I'm really disappointed in all of you. I'll talk to you boys tomorrow.

The boys get up without a word and leave. Mrs. Lewis sits down at her desk and sighs.

Mrs. Lewis: (To herself) What can I do? Give them all F's, call their parents in for conferences, go to the principal—how can I handle it? They said my tests were too hard, . . . but that doesn't justify their cheating—nothing does!

The cheaters **95**

MRS. LEWIS' GRADEBOOK

Subject: American history

* = student who cheated.
+ = student who informed.

Month
Date
Names

Names	Quiz	Test	Homework	Quiz	Test	Homework
Adams, Jeffrey	B	B	C	C	C	B
Ashly, Richard	D	D	D	D	F	D
Atterbury, Jamie	C	C	B	C	C	C
Bailey, Jimmy	B	C	B	C	C	C
Black, Timmy	A	A	A	B	A	A
Bunch, John *	D	A	F	F	A	D
Dale, Wendy	C	C	B	C	B	C
Ernst, Timmy	C	C	C	C	C	C
Faraway, Rick	A	B	A	A	B	A
Farmer, Patty	C	C	C	C	C	C
George, Susie +	B	C	B	C	C	B
Gilbert, Shannon	A	A	B	A	A	A
Haines, Betty	B	B	B	B	C	B
Hubert, Ellis	C	D	C	D	C	D
Jackson, April	F	D	F	D	D	F
James, Mary	C	C	C	C	C	C
Johnson, Joe	D	C	D	D	D	C
Krieger, Sam *	D	B	D	F	A	F
Kristy, Linda	B	C	B	B	C	B
Largo, Kent *	F	B	F	D	A	F
Litchfield, William	C	C	C	C	C	C

Name							
Martin, Carl	B	C	B	C	C	C	B
Moore, Cathy	D	D	C	C	D	D	C
Mottola, Diane	C	D	D	D	D	C	C
Murry, Calvin	C	A	F	F	A	D	D
Nisner, Paul *	F	D	F	D	D	A	D
Nopworth, Greg	D	D	F	D	D	D	D
Page, Carolyn	B	C	B	C	B	B	B
Pellis, Robert	C	C	B	C	C	C	C
Quincy, Burt	A	B	B	B	B	B	B
Rawis, Philip	F	F	F	D	D	D	D
Simmons, Joey *	F	A	D	F	A	A	B
Snyder, Mark +	B	C	C	B	B	B	B
Tanner, Jim +	C	C	C	B	C	C	C
Tompson, Virginia	B	B	B	C	B	B	B
Vickers, Sally	C	D	C	C	C	C	D
Wells, Cris	B	C	B	B	C	C	B
Wilson, Sara	C	D	C	C	D	D	C

Questions—"The cheaters"

1. Why did the cheaters cheat on their history exam?
2. Has the teacher contributed to the group's desire to cheat? In what ways?
3. Why did the three honest students tell Mrs. Lewis about the cheating? Why didn't Jim join the cheaters?
4. Do the cheaters hold values and attitudes that are different from those of the students that turned them in? Whatever your answer, how do you account for the differences in their behavior?
5. In what ways do the home, the school, and the adolescent peer group foster cheating?
6. Do value inconsistencies exist in the American culture concerning cheating? For example, does our culture say, "Honesty is the best policy" on the one hand and, "If you don't look out for yourself, no one is going to" on the other? Does the American value system emphasize honesty or not getting caught? Is there a dominant set of values concerning cheating? How large a segment of the population behaves as though they believe that cheating is always wrong no matter what the circumstances?
7. What should Mrs. Lewis do about the problem? How can she prevent similar problems from arising in the future? Is there any kind of information that she could gather before deciding what to do? Should she attempt to deal with the problem herself or refer it to a disciplinary officer?

Half and half

A group of teenagers sit watching a basketball game in the gymnasium of the only high school in a midwestern city of around 50,000 population. Some are drinking cokes; some are eating candy bars and popcorn. The teenagers are all yelling enthusiastically. At the same time, Miss Bell walks into the principal's office in the main building next to the gym. She talks to the principal's secretary.

Miss Bell: I came to pick up my supplies.

Secretary: Go right in. Mrs. Adams is handing them out right now.

Miss Bell walks into a smaller inner office where the principal is handing out some supplies to another teacher. The other teacher leaves.

Mrs. Adams: (Looking up) Oh, there you are, Jane. How are things going in preparation for your first day with us?

Miss Bell: Fine, I guess. I still have to think up something bright and cheery for our bulletin board display.

Mrs. Adams: You seem real enthusiastic. (Smiling) Well, most new teachers do. (Handing Miss Bell some papers) Oh, here's the information you wanted on your junior English classes: the IQs and grades of all the 175 students you will have. Don't tell the other teachers that I had Mary get all of these for you, or they will want her to do it for them too.

Miss Bell sits at her desk in her classroom. The room is in disarray.

There are potted plants set out on one desk, a pile of posters on another, and the bulletin board display is only partially completed. A stapler, some glue, some tape, and pencils are spread out in preparation for finishing the colorful display. Miss Bell is looking over the papers that she got from the principal.

Miss Bell: (To herself) About half of these students are above average in intelligence and grades. Take William here. He's made almost straight A's in English and has an IQ of 135. But then there is Mary. The other half are about on her level or a little lower. She's made D's in English. Her IQ is 87 and some are lower than that. What a diversified class! I will really have to think of something to bridge these differences in ability. That won't be easy with 35 students in the class.

Several days later Miss Bell is lecturing about William Blake.

Miss Bell: And so, this *Introduction to Songs of Innocence* by William Blake is Blake's account of how he came to write his poems. His "cloud child" commanded and he obeyed. It makes a lovely picture in reading.
Bob: I don't understand how a ghost could tell him what to do. (Class laughs)
Bill: It wasn't a ghost, dummy. The cloud child means inspiration.
Miss Bell: Yes, Bill, you could call it that.
Mary: But what does "stain the water clear" mean?
Bill: (Retorting) He made ink, duh!

Mary blushes with embarrassment. Class laughs. Some students stare into space; some are flipping through the book looking at other selections. Some look at Miss Bell with confused faces.

Bill: Miss Bell, can't we go on to another poem? I'm tired of this stuff and. . . .

Over a month later, Miss Bell has Mary reading from Romeo and Juliet.

Mary: Juliet: How camest thou hither, tell me, and wherefore? The orchard walls are high and hard to climb, And the place death, considering who thou art, If any of my kinsmen find thee here.

Mary reads in a monotone, stumbling over words, especially the old English. The class is fidgety. Two students have their heads down. One is openly reading a library book. There is a buzz in the back of the room which eventually breaks into laughter, interrupting the reading. Miss Bell walks to the back of the room.

Miss Bell: What is all the laughter about? (Earnestly) Juliet is very serious here. Romeo could be killed by coming to see her. Do any of you re-member why? (Students exhibit blank faces; one boy tries to hide a motor magazine, but Miss Bell sees it) Is this magazine part of our class literature?

James: No, ma'am. But I don't understand what Mary's trying to read up there, anyhow.

Miss Bell: But you have disrupted the whole class. I think the Dean of Boys will need an explanation of why you are reading that magazine in class. (Other students show rebellious looks)

James: But what about Susan up there reading a library book?

Class: (Echoing) Yeah!

Susan: (Retorting quickly and cuttingly) Well, I make A's in this class; you're failing. (Class breaks into a bedlam of comments)

Miss Bell: Just a minute! This is a classroom, not a riot! Quiet down! (The class quiets down as Miss Bell continues to speak) Now, Mary, will you go on with your reading. You're doing fine.

Mary: (Shyly) But I don't understand a word I'm reading. . . .

Bell rings to signal end of class. The students get up, slamming books about and talking loudly. They walk out into the hall talking about the incident in class.

George: But, why can't she ever explain anything? She goes so fast you'd think we knew Shakespeare like we know basketball.

Sharon: (Poorly dressed) Who cares about stupid old Romeo and Juliet anyway? My older sister and her boyfriend, Pete, went to see the movie and they said they couldn't understand a word. Shakespeare is such a drag!

Mary: (Catches up with them) Do you know what Bill just asked Miss Bell? (They shake their heads) He asked why we have to spend so much time on Romeo and Juliet. He wanted something harder like . . . oh, I can't think of the name of the play, but it was another one of Shakespeare's. Can you believe he would have the nerve? (Disbelief on all faces)

Miss Bell sits in her classroom composing a letter to the parents of her slow students. She finishes the letter and reads it over for errors.

Dear Parent,
Some of the students in my class are having difficulty with the material I present each day. Therefore, I am setting up a tutoring hour every afternoon from 3:20 to 4:20 for anyone who wants help. I hope that if your child is having difficulties he will take this opportunity to go over our day's assignment, classwork, and discussions. This way I can give individual help and the problems should be ironed out. Please urge your child to come. Thank you for your consideration.

Sincerely,

Miss Jane Bell
Junior English Class
Claremont-Sims High School

Miss Bell: (To herself) I hope this will clear up the problems I've been having.

Miss Bell is in her empty classroom after school. She is sitting at her desk as two students enter.

Miss Bell: Hi, girls, have a seat. We'll just wait a few minutes until more of the students arrive.

The girls sit down and talk to each other. Two boys stand at the door. Miss Bell motions for them to come in.

Miss Bell: Come on in, boys.

Jeff: No, thanks, we just wanted to see if John and George were here. We're going to basketball practice.

The boys leave as three other girls come into the room and sit down. Two boys come in a moment later. Miss Bell looks at the clock. It is 3:30.

Miss Bell: It's time for us to begin. Do any of you have any questions? (One girl raises her hand)

It is the afternoon of the next day. The clock shows 3:30. Two students are there for the tutoring session.

Miss Bell: Well, we must begin. We'll try to help stragglers catch up when they arrive.

Mary: Oh, the boys aren't coming today. They thought we were going to have Cokes at the last session and talk about something they were interested in like basketball. What did you think of that game last night?

Judy: Yeah, Gary Clark made 35 points!

Miss Bell: Well, that's fine. But let's get down to a discussion of any problems that you might have in English.

It is refreshment time at the monthly PTA meeting and the teachers are socializing with the parents. Miss Bell is talking with one of the parents.

Miss Bell: Why didn't Mary continue to come to my tutoring sessions? I know she is having problems and the sessions would have helped a lot.

Mother: (Shaking her head) I'm sorry. I told her she'd regret it, but she said she didn't want to spend another hour at school; and I couldn't make her stay. Kids need to relax too, you know!

The next day Miss Bell visits the curriculum supervisor in his office. She sits across from him at his desk.

Miss Bell: So you see, I've tried to help by having a tutoring session each afternoon. That didn't work. Then I changed the gearing of my teaching from the average–fast to the average–slow. But now the fast students are really bored and some discipline problems have developed. I've even tried putting them in discussion groups, both fast and slow together, but that just causes pandemonium. (She pauses) Isn't there any way some of the slower students can be transferred to an easier section?

Supervisor: We don't have fast or slow classes in the school, Jane. There just aren't enough facilities to do it or we would. Anyway, almost half the year is over, and the adjustment to another class might cause even more problems.

Miss Bell: Well, then how can I gear my class to keep the fast students interested and not lose the slow ones? How do you teach a class like that?

CLAREMONT-SIMS HIGH SCHOOL

English III, 3rd Period, Miss Bell

Name	IQ	Grade, English I	Grade, English II
Acton, Mary	87	D	D
Balfe, Constance	90	D	D
Beardsley, James	76	D	D
Bush, George	82	D	D
Clark, Gary	130	A	A
Compton, Susan	125	B	A
Dale, Jeff	82	D	D
Dyer, Ribba	134	A	A
Ellis, William	135	A	A
Fechner, Robert	79	D	D
Gage, David	118	B	A
Hamilton, Charles	115	B	B
Jacobs, John	90	D	D
Johnson, Carl	85	D	D
Jones, Linda	139	A	A
Kane, Elizabeth	89	C	D
Kelly, Catherine	119	A	B
Kilpatrick, Ransom	81	D	D
Kruger, Paul	140	A	A
Lamb, John	98	D	C
Lawrence, Peggy	137	A	A
Lowell, Judith	87	D	D
Mawson, Douglas	90	D	C
Napier, Dennis	136	A	A
Ney, Mia	129	A	A

Questions—"Half and half"

1. What is a slow learner? Are slow learners mentally retarded? Are they under-achievers?
2. Are the fast students in Miss Bell's class gifted? Are they overachievers?
3. What is special education? Should Miss Bell's slow learners be in a special education class?
4. If changes could be made in the school, would it be desirable to put the fast and slow students into separate classes; that is, group them homogeneously according to their abilities? What special facilities would be required to do so?
5. What differences seem to exist between the interests of the slow learners as compared to those of the fast learners? Do they seem to share any common interests?
6. What differences seem to exist between individuals in the two groups with regard to the ways in which they perceive the classroom situation? The teacher? Themselves? One another? Literature? Do they share any common perceptions?
7. Why didn't the majority of the slow learners show up for Miss Bell's tutoring sessions?
8. Is it possible for Miss Bell to motivate both the fast and slow learners at the same time? Is motivation internal or external to the learner? Do differences exist between fast and slow learners with regard to motivation?
9. Would failing the slow students help to motivate them? What about the fast students?
10. Should Miss Bell have sent James to the Dean of Boys? Is James a discipline problem?
11. What kinds of classroom activities can Miss Bell utilize to motivate both the fast and slow learners? Should she attempt to gear her teaching to either group? Is it possible for her to gear it to individuals; that is, individualize instruction? Is the notion of a teacher determining and taking into consideration the individual differences of 35 students a realistic one?

The grading crisis

Jackson High School sits on a gentle hill overlooking the spacious, tree-lined, and immaculately kept acreage surrounding the school. The school was built at considerable expense. Jackson High is located in an upper middle-class suburb in a city of 70,000 in an eastern state. The school's tax base is one of the richest in the state. Teacher turnover is very low and salaries in the school district are among the highest in the nation. The school is 15 years old, but looks brand new. Two years ago the school board called a city referendum and won overwhelming support for a new wing of classroom buildings, a new gymnasium, and a new science laboratory. The corridors are freshly painted and several skylights were added to give the inside a bright, fresh look. The chief improvement to the exterior has been the sand blasting of the bricks and new shrubbery to outline the front of the building, making the building look deceptively new.

Ann Thompson is one of the youngest teachers at Jackson. She has taught science here for 3 years. Typically her classes are composed of bright college-bound students (96 percent of the students at Jackson go to college). Ann feels that, for the most part, her students have been fun to teach. However, recently Ann has been greatly disturbed by the growing student activism in the school—especially in her room. Sally Reynolds, a senior teacher who has been teaching trigonometry for 15 years at Jackson, has stopped by Ann Thompson's room for an after school visit.

Ann: You know, Sally, I used to be really sympathetic to students. I voted in the faculty meeting to allow students to wear arm bands lamenting the deaths at Kent State and I have always chaperoned dances and all-night senior parties. (With firmness) But I'm really disturbed about their current attitude.

Sally: Are you still upset that the students challenged your grading assignments yesterday?

Ann: (With surprise) How did you know?

Sally: Well, from what I hear you were talking about your grade crisis quite a bit in the lounge this morning. You should know that anything said in the lounge spreads pretty quickly—especially if it's a problem that other teachers might have to face. I came in today to hear about this incident from you.

Ann: You know Bill Meyers?

Sally: The star athlete?

Ann: (Nodding) The same. The star athlete, the student council president, the Cambodia-Vietnam critic, the concerned student. (Said with a rising voice)

Sally: (Kiddingly) Ann, you sound like a biased reporter—"Just give me the facts, ma'am." What happened?

Ann: (Blushing) Thanks, Sally. I guess I am up-tight, as the students say. (Laughing) I'll tell you what led to this condition. Yesterday I gave a C to Bill Meyers on an exam. It's the first C he's gotten in this course and he couldn't accept it; he started to accuse me of being an unfair grader. He. . . . (Sally breaks her off)

Sally: Oh, come on, Ann. I have been a teacher here for 15 years. Quit sermonizing and tell me what actually happened.

Ann: Sally, you make me feel like I'm being cross-examined.

Sally: (In a kinder manner) I'm sorry, Ann, but I have heard this discussed four times today and I still don't know what happened. This is serious business with many long-range ramifications for the school. Bill Meyers, at least in my class, has always been a gentleman and a good student. His father is on the school board and he is a serious, fair-minded man. I know that he called our principal this morning and the principal has called a meeting of the senior staff. You know I like you, but I want to know what actually happened so we can deal with the problem. I want to help you.

Ann: (Mollified) Okay! I gave the test back—It was the fourth test in the semester. I put the distribution of the scores on the board and placed the cut-off marks for A, B, C, and D scores. Bill had the highest C in the room. As I remember, Bill raised his hand and when I called on him he politely asked, "Miss Thompson, how can you tell the difference between an A and a B?" I said something like, "Bill, it's hard to give a precise answer, but I try to find large and real intervals between student test performances. I look at the distribution for *real* differences and use a very loose, informal curve." Then Bill said, "But look at the gaps between the A's and B's, and between the B's and C's. Eight points separate the A's and the B's, but only four points separate the B's and C's. Look at the students getting A's. Their scores range from 100 to

93—a difference of seven points! But you say that a difference of only four points from the lowest B makes my paper a C. Is that fair?" He then placed on the board the distribution of grades from the preceding test and pointed out the discrepancy of grades between the two tests. He then suggested that there was nothing real in my grading and said I was just grading on relative competition.

Sally: (In a serious and intense manner) Did you ask Bill or the class how they would grade the set of scores? How they would go about making real divisions in grading that are fair to everyone?

Ann: (Shaking her head slowly) No. I was too frustrated to think of anything rational like that. I don't know what happened after that except at last in exasperation I shouted at Bill telling him that he was questioning the grades because he had done poorly.

Sally: You blamed him because you didn't know how to explain your grading?

Ann: (Nodding) Yes, I guess so. But he was humiliating me. He embarrassed me.

Sally: (Serious and intense) You and I both know how much pressure is put on these students for good grades. I think that we also know that they are bright, good kids but we do expect them to do a great deal of work and their parents want them in the best colleges. That means good grades or else. These kids may get away with a lot, but poor school work is one thing their parents really clamp down on. A couple of C's and they lose their car privileges and anything else that's fun. (She continues earnestly) Look, Ann, what I'm saying is that Bill Meyers wasn't just taking you on. He was attacking the system—the pressure.

Ann: (Smiling) Sally, I feel better now. Thanks for stopping. . . . (Sally breaks in)

Sally: (Frowning and shaking her head negatively) Wish I could leave you feeling better, but I've got to give you some bad news. This afternoon at student government, Bill plans to submit a bill asking teachers to state *explicitly* the basis on which they assign grades.

Ann: (Musingly) I had no idea that he felt that strongly.

Sally: Apparently he does. The motion will come up for a vote next week. Ann, I think it would be a good idea for you to talk with the class about grading. Tell them what you are doing and get their reactions and suggestions.

Ann: (Pleadingly) But how? That's my problem. We sure never covered grading in any of the education courses that I took in college and the school here hasn't given me any guidelines. I don't know of any other ways to assign grades. What can I do?

DISTRIBUTION OF SCORES IN MISS THOMPSON'S CLASS: TEST 3 AND TEST 4

Test 3		Test 4	
87		100	
86	A's	98	
85		97	A's
81 (Bill's score)		96	
———		95	
78		94	
77		93	
76		———	
75	B's	85	
74		84	
73		84	B's
73		84	
73		83	
73		82	
———		———	
65		78 (Bill's score)	
65		77	
65		77	
65		76	C's
65	C's	75	
64		74	
63		73	
62		———	
62		69	
62		68	D's
———		67	
		———	

Questions—"The grading crisis"

1. In determining grades, should the teacher: (A) compare the student's performance to that of other studetns; (B) compare the student's performance to a standard of performance determined (probably in advance of the test) by the teacher; (C) compare the student's performance to his own past performance; (D) use a combination of the above; (E) vary the type of comparison made according to the instructional objectives being pursued?
2. What is a normal curve and how can it be used in assigning grades? What assumptions are made when a normal curve is used?
3. What is a calculated curve? How does it differ from a normal curve? What are standard scores and how can they be used to assign grades?
4. What is percentage grading and how does it differ from normal and calculated curve grading?
5. Should students be graded on effort? Can student effort be determined by comparing a student's grade with the grade that he made on the same or similar test in the past?
6. Is it true that our society is a competitive one? What grading procedures seem best suited to prepare a student to live in our society?
7. Do the needs of middle-class parents and students put pressure on teachers to give objective-type tests and to assign grades on a group comparison basis utilizing "statistically-sanctified" techniques for deciding where to draw the line that divides one grade from another?
8. Should schools have explicit grading guidelines for teachers to follow or would such guidelines be a violation of academic freedom and, in the long run, do more harm than good?
9. Should grades be abolished entirely in the public schools? Should a pass-fail grading system be substituted for the traditional one?
10. Should students be involved in determining grades? Should they be permitted to determine other students' grades? Can the individual student be trusted to make the final determination of his own grade?
11. How should grades be determined in schools which assign students to classes on the basis of ability-grouping procedures? Should the grades in a low-ability class generally not go above a C and those in a high-ability class generally not fall below a C?
12. How would you assign grades to the distribution of scores for Test 3 and Test 4?
13. What should Miss Thompson do? How should she approach the class and Bill Meyers?

Corky: drop-out or cop-out?

It is almost 8:30 A.M. on a cold, wind-swept day in a midwestern state. The school, which was an old factory building converted into a junior high school, stands bleakly outlined against a gray sky. It is located in a district of low-income families, mostly factory and blue-collar workers. Most of the children have already entered the building, but a few late-comers are hastily making their way up the long flight of steps to the entrance.

The last two to enter the building are 15-year-old boys. They walk down the narrow hall together, talking casually on their way to their ninth-grade art class. Vic, the taller and more slender boy, is wearing a windbreaker over an army surplus shirt and jeans. He has a heavy Maltese cross around his neck. His hair is long and shows fading signs of once being peroxided. He seems to slide along on his heel taps.

Vic: Hey, Corky! Seen your brother out in front of school just now. Sure has got his car looking good. He's really got it made, working out there at Jim's DX Station. He can really live now. (Said with a wistful note)

Corky is shorter and huskier than Vic, but well proportioned. He is wearing tight jeans with a wide, imitation leather belt, boots, and a worn leather jacket. His face is pleasant, and his manner cordial.

Corky: Yeah, Jim's got it knocked. He's pulling down $200 a month and all he has to do is fill cars and talk to the other guys. What a soft job! (He adds, proudly) I go down there every night. Say, you wanna meet me after school tonight and go with me? It'll be okay with Jim.

Vic: Neat. (He grins in affirmation) See you about 7:00. Okay?

They enter a large, cluttered room where over 30 other students have gathered. Most of the students are aimlessly milling around before the last bell rings. A few stand examining the drawings which line the dingy green walls. There are 7 or 8 spindly easels scattered at random around the room. Most of the desks are covered with stacks of paper in disarray and half-empty jars of tempera paint. Corky puts his books on his desk and walks back to the teacher's desk. The teacher is a young woman, not more than six years older than the members of the class. She is busy collecting the painting supplies from the cabinet beside her desk.

Corky: (Pleasantly) Hi, Miss McInnis. What are we going to do today?

Miss McInnis: (She looks up) Oh, hi, Corky. We're going to do landscapes.

Corky: What do you mean, landscapes?

Miss McInnis: You know, Corky. Pictures of the outdoors—mountains, trees, streams, that kind of thing.

Corky: Oh, yeah. (Pause) Do you want me to help with those paint brushes? You look like you've got your hands full.

Miss McInnis: Why, thanks, Corky. That would be a real help. Make sure everyone has one. (She adds, firmly) And make sure everyone gives one *back* at the end of the class, too!

The bell rings as she finishes her collection of the supplies and turns to the students who have casually taken their seats.

Miss McInnis: Today, class, we're going to paint landscapes.

Girl in the back: (In a loud voice) You mean we're going outside? Today?

Miss McInnis: No, no, we're going to work from memory. Remember going on a picnic to the state park with your family and. . . .

Vic: (With sarcasm) You've got to be kidding! My old man would never take me on a stupid picnic!

The other members of the class look at each other and roll their eyes before bursting into laughter.

Miss McInnis: (Raising her voice) Class, that'll be enough. (The laughter dies as she continues) Just think of the outdoors. I'm sure you've seen a tree before. Now, let's work.

The class becomes disruptive as soon as Miss McInnis turns and leaves the front of the room. Everyone starts up to the faucet at the same time to get water for their paints.

Miss McInnis: (Loudly) Oh, no! Just one at a time, please!

Miss McInnis begins to walk around looking at the painting progress.

She stops by Corky's desk. He is using colors straight from the box and is working in broad strokes. He is totally engrossed in his work.

Miss McInnis: Corky, why don't you vary your colors? Look, if you add a little yellow to this green, it will lighten up your grass. Remember the lesson we had last week on mixing colors?

Miss McInnis mixes the paint and on another sheet shows Corky different ways to get these colors.

Corky: (With admiration) Say, that's neat, Miss McInnis. Sure looks better this way, doesn't it? (He pauses) Did you take lots of art in school?

Miss McInnis: Yes, I did. I went to college to learn to be an art teacher. It took me four years.

Corky: Four years! Gee whiz, that's a lot of time just to be something.

Vic has been listening intently to the exchange between Corky and Miss McInnis.

Vic: Yeah, my pop says college is a waste of money. All people do in college is sit around and read books and waste taxpayers' money. Kids are just avoiding the draft.

The class continues to paint with sporadic interest and much discussion among themselves. One boy flips paint on another and is sent to the principal's office. Soon he returns.

Miss McInnis: Tom, what did the principal say?

Tom pulls out a sheet of paper torn from a coloring book and puts it on the teacher's desk. He is smiling broadly.

Tom: He said that if I was going to act like a baby, I should do baby work. (He starts to laugh)

The class hears this exchange and breaks into hearty laughter. Corky walks over to the paper on the teacher's desk and picks it up to display to the class.

Miss McInnis: (With exasperation) Corky, sit down. There are enough troublemakers in this class already. I don't need you too!

Corky: (Good-naturedly) Aw, come on, Miss McInnis. It's just a joke.

Miss McInnis: (Wearily) It's almost time for the period to end. Please clean up. (Corky picks up the paint brushes and brings them back to the desk)

Corky: Miss McInnis, can we work with that clay stuff tomorrow? I like that.

Miss McInnis: Maybe, Corky. We'll see.

It is noon of the following day. The students are eating in the combination lunchroom-auditorium. The teachers have a separate eating lounge. Miss McInnis is talking to two older teachers.

Miss McInnis: That ninth-grade class is going to be the end of me. I think they're all juvenile delinquents. The only one that even acknowledges my presence is Corky Roberts, and he's one of the few who ever completes anything. The others are constantly throwing things. And yesterday, this one girl literally cussed Vic out! (She adds ruefully) Not that he didn't deserve it! (Her voice softens) Doris, you had Corky last year. Was he as nice in your class?

Doris Smith is the history teacher. She is in her early 30s, and she gives the impression of maturity and competence.

Doris: Well, Ellen, I'll admit you've got the worst bunch in school. Corky is a dear, though. At first I thought he was trying to be overly pleasant just to get a good grade, but after one term when I just *had* to give him a D, he was just as friendly and pleasant as ever. Frankly, I really hated to give him a D. . . . (Half to herself) He did an excellent project. It was a beautiful bas-relief map of one of the countries we'd been studying. (She adds, with a shake of her head) But his final exam was miserable! And you know, I think he couldn't have cared less about his grade. Evidently, no one looks at his report card at home, and his brothers certainly aren't any inspiration to him! (Miss Sledd, a veteran teacher of English, chimes in)

Miss Sledd: I know only too well what you mean. I've had his two brothers and I have Corky now. His brother Jim was a real terror. You might as well talk to the wall. I think he quit school last year after he turned 16. But, now, Corky could make it. He acts as if he enjoys my class, but he *never* applies himself.

Mrs. Smith: Do you suppose he just isn't very bright? He always asked so many questions I just assumed he was bright enough. (She smiles lamely) Funny, it's so reassuring to know that *someone* is listening, you forget to wonder whether his questions are good ones or not!

Miss Sledd: I'd been wondering whether Corky's capable or not . . . but his record shows his last IQ score to be 108. With an IQ like that he should never make below a C. (She adds) But I'll just bet that he quits school soon.

Miss McInnis: Have you ever talked to his parents?

Miss Sledd: I called his mother once. She works all day and his father doesn't live with them. She said Corky was a big boy and could do what he wanted. She was too busy to come in to talk about him.

Miss McInnis: I really hate to see him quit, don't you?

It is the morning of the next day. The students in Miss McInnis' first-period art class rush in right before the bell. Vic punches Corky playfully on the arm and one boy throws a girl's purse up front.

Miss McInnis: Class, please, let's settle down. Today we are going to break into groups and work on projects. Some will work on a mural and some can work with clay. How many want to work on the mural?

Three students raise their hands. When Miss McInnis asks who wants to work with clay, four raise their hands. Corky is wildly waving his arm, almost jumping out of his seat.

Miss McInnis: Well, what do the other 20 want to do? Fingerpaint?

This brings hysterical laughter and the students begin yelling, "Let me!" "No, me!" "Yeah, let's fingerpaint like the primer kids." Miss McInnis finally quiets them down and most of the students begin to work. In the back room which houses the clay wheel, Corky is working on his pot. Miss McInnis walks back to check on his progress.

Miss McInnis: Say, Corky, that's pretty good.

Corky: Yeah, I like this, too. (They both watch for a long minute as his pot takes form) Say, Miss McInnis, my brother is having a party this weekend, and I wondered if you'd help me make something.

Miss McInnis: Well, what did you have in mind?

Corky: I want to make some big beer mugs for my brother to use for his parties. (With pride) All my brother's friends get together and have parties all the time. Man, ever since my brother and his buddies dropped out of school, they sure have a blast.

Miss McInnis: Corky, do you plan to quit school, too?

Corky: Sure! I can get a job working at the station where my brother does. I can make good money and buy my own car.

Miss McInnis: But, Corky, you should finish school. Don't drop out now!

Corky: Why not? I'm not going to college anyway.

CUMULATIVE RECORD

Tatum Junior High School

Name: Roberts, Corky Joe
Address: 428 Pine Street
Father: Joe H. Roberts
Mother: Rose C. Roberts
Siblings: Jim A., Age 17, Homer C., Age 16

Home phone: 734-0738
Occupation: Laborer
Occupation: Factory Employee

Former school: Hodges Elementary
Date entered:
General health: Good
Handicaps: None
Date of birth: January 24, 1954

TEST RECORD

Form	IQ	Date	Grade
Alpha	111	10-14-63	3
Beta	104	10-21-67	7
Gamma	108	10-16-70	9

INTELLIGENCE TESTS:
Otis Quick-Scoring
Mental Ability Tests

ACADEMIC RECORD

Grades 7-9 (year averages)

Grade 7		Grade 8		Grade 9
Eng.	C	Eng.	C	
Geog.	C	U.S. Hist.	D	
Arith.	D	Arith.	D	
P.E.	A	P.E.	A	
Band	B	Band	B	

Personal and Social Development
Code: 1—Superior; 5—Unsatisfactory

Grade	7	8
Initiative	4	4
Integrity	3	3
Leadership	4	4
Social Attitude	2	2
Emotional Stability	3	3

Grades 1-6 (year averages)

	1	2	3	4	5	6
Citizenship	A	A	A	B	B	B
Lang. Arts	B	B	B	B	B	B
Reading	B	B	B	B	C	C
English		B	B	B	C	C
Spelling	B	B	B	C	C	C
Writing	A	A	B	B	B	B
Social Studies		B	B	C	C	C
Arithmetic	B	B	C	C	D	D
Music	B	B	B	B	B	B

Questions—"Corky: drop-out or cop-out?"

1. Into what social class does Corky seem to have been born? What values does this social class seem to hold concerning education?
2. What are values and how are they learned? Under what conditions do they change? What values does Corky seem to hold concerning education? How did he probably obtain them?
3. Is it fair to say that Corky is imitating his brothers? Under what conditions does imitation take place? Is imitating different from modeling and identifying? Under what conditions do human beings stop imitating a model? Why do they choose a given model to imitate?
4. Does the school's curriculum seem to be relevant to Corky's needs?
5. Does Corky seem to be learning in school? What is he learning? Is there a difference between learning and achievement? Is Corky achieving? What relationship exists between IQ and achievement? Between IQ and learning? IQ and intelligence? IQ and self-concept? IQ and creativity? IQ and problem-solving?
6. In Corky's case, is there likely to be transfer of learning from the classroom to the life that he is likely to lead? What about the transfer value of what he is learning in Miss McInnis' art class?
7. Is Corky exercising his free will as a human being if he decides to quit school? What forces have probably operated on him up to this point in his life to somewhat limit the range of choices open to him? Is he truly free to choose to become whatever he wants to be, even the President of the United States, or is only one choice really open to him at this point even though the teacher seems to be holding the illusion that others are open to him? That is, is his fate predetermined by the culture into which he has been born?
8. What should Miss McInnis say or do about the statement that Corky makes at the end concerning his future? What can Miss McInnis, the rest of the school personnel, and for that matter all educators do about potential drop-outs? Why do most drop-outs occur? What changes can be made in education to help deal with this problem?

The stay-in problem

Steve Rogers is 21 years old and is beginning his first year of teaching English in grades 7–12. The school in which he teaches is located in the city of Greenville, which has a population of around 5000 and is situated in the northern portion of one of the southern border states. Coal mining and agriculture are the chief contributors to the local economy although the town merchants outnumber other economic groups on the school board.

The school system is consolidated and includes about half of the county population. Greenville has had 4 superintendents in the last 10 years. Financial support of the Greenville Public Schools is about average for the size of the population being served. The junior high school is composed of grades 7 and 8 and is in the same building as the 4-year high school.

Greenville High School is located in a square-shaped building constructed of brick and wood in the 1930s. Its floors are wooden and the seats are bolted to the floor. The walls of the room are green and the furniture is old and dark brown. Both the building and its equipment are well maintained. All the desks have been recently sanded and painted to remove carvings on their surfaces.

Steve sits in the office of the principal, John Sawyer, a bald man in his 50s. The first faculty meeting of the year has just ended a few minutes before.

Mr. Sawyer: Steve, I have a problem that I'm going to ask you to help me with. (Steve leans forward in his chair) As you probably know, we were expecting Mrs. Dixon to teach social studies for us this fall until we found out that she was pregnant. I've been able to get all of her courses covered except for a world history class. (Leans forward and speaks warmly) Steve, I know that English is your field but I noticed on your credentials that you took some history courses when you were in college. Will you help me out by taking the class for me this year? We probably won't be able to get a qualified replacement for Mrs. Dixon until next year.

Steve: (Hesitantly) I'd be glad to help in any way that I can, Mr. Sawyer, but world history is really out of my field. Those history courses that I took as a sophomore were in United States history. (Reluctantly) I'll give it a try if you want me to but I'm afraid that some of the kids will know more about history than I do.

Mr. Sawyer: (Smiling) I don't think that there's much danger of that, Steve. They are just average sophomores like the students that you'll have in your English 10 sections. In fact, I'd be greatly surprised if that bright group of kids you have in your third-period English 8 section didn't challenge you a heck of a lot more than these kids. Most of the students in your history class are C students. (Stands up) Well, Steve, since you're doing me a favor, I'm going to fix the schedule so you won't have to take a study hall this year. I know that you'll be able to use the planning time. (Smiles again, then becomes serious) If you have any trouble with the history class, talk to Ray Clark (Chairman of the Social Studies Department). I've asked him to help you out.

Steve: (Stands up) Thanks, Mr. Sawyer. I'll do my best and hope that I can keep at least a page ahead of them.

Mr. Sawyer: I hope that you know that I really appreciate your helping me out of this spot. Just keep on top of them and you won't have any trouble. Be firm at first and you can loosen up on them later on. Move them along at whatever pace you want to set.

The fourth-period (11:05 A.M.–12:00 A.M.) world history class meets for the first time. Steve's classroom has a picture of Shakespeare on the wall and a set of wall maps related to English literature. At one side of the classroom sits a stand containing a set of world history maps that Ray Clark has loaned to Steve. The 34 sophomores become quiet as Steve begins to talk.

Steve: (Smiling, as he paces) I guess it's no secret that history isn't exactly my field. But English and history are very closely related to one another. People who make history often write books—and if they don't write them they are very much influenced by them. (A tall, athletically built boy in the front row holds up his hand) Yes?

Larry: What are we going to have to do in here?

Steve: What's your name? (Steve sits down on top of his desk with a serious look on his face)

Larry: Larry Zuk.

Steve: (Sternly) Well, Larry, we're going to read and discuss history. Studying history is like studying anything else—it's hard work. Read each assignment that I make carefully before you come to class. That way the class discussions will be a lot more meaningful to you. (He concludes, firmly) Yes? (Steve looks at a girl in the back row who has held up her hand)

Girl: What kind of tests will we have?

Steve: They will mostly be essay, although we'll probably have some short-answer quizzes once a week. Oh, yes—(Pauses) each Friday I want you to bring in newspaper clippings on current events and place them on the bulletin board over there. (Steve points) Of course we'll talk about them first.

Larry: (Without raising his hand) We had to do that stuff in the eighth grade and my dad got mad at me for cutting up the newspaper. (Five other students voice their support)

Steve: (Loudly) Quiet down, all of you. Larry, when you have something to say raise your hand like everyone else. (Larry smirks) You just tell your parents that the newspaper clippings are part of your school work and you won't have any trouble.

It is one week later. Steve and Ray Clark sit alone in Ray's room after school. Social studies maps, charts, and diagrams are in evidence all around the classroom. A large bulletin board contains several pictures and newspaper clippings. A large picture of John F. Kennedy hangs on the wall above Ray's desk.

Ray: Which kids are giving you the most trouble?

Steve: Larry Zuk, George Ramey, Kenneth Stone, Jack Dickinson, Larry Gage, and—uh—Sam—uh. . . .

Ray: Sam Agar?

Steve: Yeah, Sam Agar.

Ray: (Nodding) I know that group well. They have been causing trouble since grade school. What have they been doing?

Steve: Just smarting off, mostly. You know—asking cute questions, speaking out without holding up their hands, and Larry Zuk got up yesterday while I was talking and sharpened his pencil. I was so surprised that I let him get away with it.

Ray: (Laughs loudly) That's Larry. (Becomes serious) Well, Steve, you're just going to have to handle them the same way their other teachers have handled them—let them know the rules and enforce them. I'll let Ed (the vice-principal) know that you'll be sending him his favorite customers. You've just got to knock a few heads! (Pauses) You know, sometimes I wonder what any of these kids really learn in high school. I guess if we can get them reading and writing we have done about all we can do.

Steve: Yes, I learned more in my first college course than I did in all four years of high school. I hope that I can teach a few of them how to study so that they can make it in college. (Pauses) Well, thanks for your help, Ray. I think that I'll go see Ed myself before I go home.

The next day Steve meets his world history class. He paces back and forth as he asks the class questions.

Steve: What is the difference between history and prehistory? Susan.

Susan: History began when man began writing things down.

Steve: How long ago was that, Susan?

Susan: (Looks down at her text) 4241 B.C. is the oldest writing that has ever been found.

Steve: Right. It was an old Egyptian calendar. Anything before that date is prehistory. (Steve looks to the back of the room where the six boys sit together as a group. George Ramey holds up his hand) Yes, George?

George: Was this building built before or after history?

Steve: (Sarcastically) Very funny, George.

Larry: Before, you dumb-dumb! We don't have any Egyptian calendars. (The whole class laughs)

Steve: (Sharply) That's enough, Larry. I've warned you once about raising your hand. (The class quiets down) Jack Dickinson, how long has man been on the earth?

Jack: We aren't going to get on that evolution bit are we, Mr. Rogers? That's against my religion.

Steve: (Smirking) What *is* your religion, Jack?

Jack: I'm an objector.

Steve: What kind of an objector?

Jack: We object to being asked questions about history. (The class laughs again)

Steve: (Loudly and with a look of anger on his face) All right, that's enough! (Class quiets down gradually; Steve speaks with controlled anger) If you guys want to play games, it's going to cost you. The next smart remark. . . .

Larry: (Quickly) Anyone for tennis?

Steve: Okay, Larry. Go to Mr. Irish's office. (Larry gets up smiling and leaves; the class quiets down) Now, unless someone else objects (Looks back at the five boys) let's get back to work. Who can tell me what artifacts are? (Pauses and looks around) No one? It was in your assigned reading for today. (Pauses, looks around, and frowns) Okay—since nobody seems to know, we'll just put it on the next test. You'd better know it by then!

It is the end of the same school day and Steve goes to Ed Irish's office. As he enters the office, Ed gets up from behind his desk.

Ed: Hi, Steve.

Steve: Hi, Ed. Did Larry Zuk come to your office the fourth period? (Steve and Ed both sit down)

Ed: Yes, he did. He told me what happened and I took him down to the boiler room and gave him three whacks. Larry and I are old buddies.

Steve: Do you think that it did any good?

Ed: I doubt it. Steve, all six of those boys will probably give you serious trouble sooner or later. The only way that I have been able to calm them down is to lay the wood to them. But now that they are 16 that doesn't work any longer. (Shakes his head) I have called their parents and expelled the boys until I am blue in the face. (With emphasis) Their parents just aren't interested. Sometimes I think that we have a stay-in problem instead of a drop-out problem in the public schools.

Steve: Those six boys ruin the class for the rest of the kids.

Ed: I know that, Steve. I'll tell you what. I don't think that it's fair of John to ask you to bail him out and then stick you with those six hoods. It won't do any good to move them into other classes either.

Steve: Dividing them won't help?

Ed: No. That's already been tried. Larry Zuk alone is so mean and tough that I hear that his parents are actually afraid of him. The other five can be just as tough as Larry.

Steve: (Smiling in disbelief) Really!

Ed: Yes. I guess Larry beat his father up bad once.

Steve: If his dad can't handle him, then how can anyone expect us to?

Ed: I agree, Steve. I guess I have reached a decision if you agree to go along with me. I will expel the boys again for three days. In the meantime, I'll tell John that the boys have disrupted another class and ask him to ask the superintendent to recommend to the board that they be permanently expelled. The boards meets tomorrow night so chances are you won't have to put up with them in class again. Okay?

Steve: I don't know, Ed. What will become of them when they are expelled? I'm not sure that they did anything bad enough in my class to warrant permanent expulsion. I. . . .

Ed: (Interrupting) Your class is just the straw that broke that camel's back. They have been disrupting this school for many years now and will probably eventually end up in the reformatory. (Pause) Tell me, Steve—do you want to keep them in your class?

Questions—"The stay-in problem"

1. What is an authoritarian personality? Does Steve have an authoritarian personality? What about Mr. Irish?
2. What is punishment? What instances of punishment can you cite in this case? Is any of Steve's behavior punishing? What relationships exist between punishment and learning? How is punishment related to frustration?
3. Is motivation the answer to discipline problems? What is a discipline problem and what is motivation? Are some subjects and some teaching methods more motivating than others?
4. Has Steve's effectiveness probably been impaired by his having to teach a course out of his field? Would you expect him to be more effective in his English classes? What do Steve's teaching objectives seem to be in world history? Does the textbook seem to constitute his curriculum and daily lesson plans? How could he have taught world history differently?
5. What relationships exist between teacher expectancies and pupil behavior? What expectations does Mr. Irish have with regard to the six boys?
6. If you could perform magic, in what ways would you change Steve? Would you change anyone else in the school? Would you change the school system and the community?
7. Would obtaining more information about the six boys help Steve decide what to do about them? If yes, what information should be gathered and from what sources? If Steve gathers more information about the boys, what would you predict that he will find out?
8. Do you agree with Mr. Irish that the schools have a stay-in problem? Would it do certain students any good to leave school, to work for awhile, and perhaps return to school later?
9. What should Steve say or do next? Can he do anything to prevent situations like this from developing in the future? If Steve decides to keep the boys in his class, what changes should he make?

Tired Ted: pass or fail?

Mike Thompson is in his first year of teaching at a high school located in a populous eastern state. The school draws its students from a primarily rural attendance area.

Inside the building (constructed in the 1940s), Mr. Thompson's seniors in problems of democracy are working in small groups on a project. Mr. Thompson is walking from group to group answering and asking questions. He stops at one group which doesn't seem to be doing anything. One boy, Ted, has his head down. A girl is combing her hair. The three other students are trying to discuss the problem.

Mr. Thompson: What's the trouble here?

Janet: We're trying to define the problem, Mr. Thompson, but as you can see, Ted and Cathy aren't too interested.

Cathy: It's just a dumb problem.

Mr. Thompson: Ted, are you asleep?

Ted: (Who hasn't moved during the whole conversation) No. (Lifts his head) I'm not asleep; I'm just bored.

Mr. Thompson: Well, you and Cathy had better get to work. Your grades depend on this project. You want to pass your senior year and graduate, don't you? (He walks away)

Ted: (Said so that only the group can hear him) I don't really care at this point.

It is the same day but Ted is now in Mr. Brook's English class. Ted has his head down on his desk.

Mr. Brook: Ted, will you stay after class a minute? I need to talk to you.

The bell rings and the class leaves. Ted saunters up to Mr. Brook's desk. Mr. Brook gets out his gradebook and traces his finger down the page to Ted's name.

Mr. Brook: One D, four F's on your tests; a D average on your themes; and an F in class participation. . . . What do you expect me to do, Ted? How can I pass you this year unless you get to work and show me that you can do something? Don't you want to pass your senior year?

Ted: Yeah, I do.

The next morning Ted's mother is seated by the principal's desk. The principal, Mr. Dale, is listening to Mrs. Stone, who seems very distraught at the moment.

Mrs. Stone: How can he be making F's in two of his classes? I can't figure it out—Ted's a good boy. Those teachers must not know Ted very well. He's made C's and D's in his other classes. That's good enough. But his father says Ted just better pass this year or he is going to talk to the school board. My husband knows most of the members and works with two of them. . . .

It is the end of the same day in Mr. Thompson's classroom and the room is empty except for Mr. Thompson who sits at his desk averaging grades. Mr. Dale comes and stands by Mike's desk as he talks to him.

Mr. Dale: Mike, Ted Stone's mother visited me today to discuss Ted's grades. She seems especially upset at his straight F's in here. Is Ted going to pass democracy? His mother got so upset that she told me her husband would go to the school board if Ted didn't graduate.

Mr. Thompson: Ted just won't do his homework. All he does in class is sleep or stare into space. I don't quite know what to do with him. Of course, with our grading system, he has a choice of his Regent's Exam, his final exam, or his year's average, whichever is highest. So maybe he still has a chance of passing. All he has to get is 65 percent on one.

Mr. Dale: Since our main concern is for the student, we should give Ted the benefit of the doubt if one exists. I know that you'll give Ted's case your usual concern.

Mr. Dale leaves. Mr. Thompson averages Ted's class grades. He records 40 percent.

Mr. Thompson: (To himself) He'll have to work a lot to bring that up. Maybe with luck he'll do well on his Regent's Exam coming up. Either that or his final exam will have to save him.

Several days later, Mr. Thompson is proctoring the state Regent's Exam. All the students are writing except Ted. When the bell rings the students pass in their tests and booklets. Ted puts a blank test on top of the stack. The students shuffle out of the room.

Mr. Thompson: (Calling) Ted. (Ted crosses over to him) You couldn't think of anything to write on this exam?

Ted: Nope. It was a dumb exam. I've still got the final.

Mr. Thompson: You'd better work hard between now and then if you want to pass for the year.

Ted: (Confidently) I'll pass, Mr. Thompson.

A few weeks later Mr. Thompson sits at his desk working on his grade-book. Ted Stone has no final grade. Mr. Thompson computes a few more final averages. Ted enters with a note in his hand.

Mr. Thompson: Well, Ted, where were you on finals day?

Ted: I was sick. I've got a note. I had a bad case of tonsillitis. Will you give me a chance to take the final? I promise I'll study. My dad is awful mad and I've just got to pass. . . .

Mr. Thompson: All right, Ted. I'll let you take a make-up exam this Thursday. That gives you three days. I hope you take my advice and really study; whether you pass depends solely now upon your final test grade.

Ted: Thanks, Mr. Thompson. See you Thursday.

It is Thursday after school. Mr. Thompson sits alone in his room and has just finished grading Ted's final exam. He marks 55 percent at the top.

Mr. Thompson: (To himself) This test result shows great improvement, but it is not a 65 percent passing mark. Ted tried, but just couldn't acquire all the information he needed in three days. If he had just done a little better on his class work or even written something on his Regent's Exam. (Pause) If I don't pass him, he won't graduate. But he really deserves not to pass. Seems like either way I go, I'll be wrong.

CUMULATIVE RECORD

Lincoln High School

Name:	Stone, Theodore Carl		Former School:	
Address:	427 Lilac place	Home phone:	367-2136	Date entered:	8-29-58
Father:	Stone, Ira J.	Occupation:	Bldg. Contractor	General health:	Excellent
Mother:	Stone, Betty G.	Occupation:	Housewife	Handicaps:	None
Siblings:	Mary A., Age 5			Date of birth:	10-14-52

TEST RECORD

INTELLIGENCE TESTS:

Otis Quick-Scoring
Mental Ability Tests

Form	IQ	Date	Grade
Alpha	102	10-14-60	3
Beta	94	10-20-64	7
Gamma	97	10-18-67	10

ACADEMIC RECORD

Grades 1-6 (year averages)

	1	2	3	4	5	6
Citizenship	C	C	C	C	C	C
Lang. Arts	C	C	C	C	C	C
Reading	C	C	C	C	C	C
English			C	C	D	D
Spelling	B	B	B	B	B	C
Writing	B	B	C	B	C	B
Social Studies			C	C	C	C
Arithmetic	B	B	C	B	C	C
Music	B	B	C	B	B	B

Grades 7-9 (year averages)

Grade 7		Grade 8		Grade 9	
Eng.	D	Eng.	C	Eng.	C
Geog.	C	U.S. Hist.	D	World	D
Arith.	D	Arith.	C	Hist.	D
P.E.	B	P.E.	A	Algebra	B
Band	B	Band	B	P.E.	D
				Spanish	D

Grades 10-12 (year averages)

Grade 10		Grade 11		Grade 12 (1st sem. only)	
Eng.	C	Eng.	D	Eng.	F
Biol.	D	Shop I	C	Shop II	C
Gen.	D	Bus.	D	Typing	D
Math	D	Mach.	C	Demo-	
Spanish	D	U.S. Hist.	D	cracy	F
P.E.	B	P.E.	B	P.E.	C

PERSONAL AND SOCIAL DEVELOPMENT

Code: 1—Superior; 5—Unsatisfactory

Grade	9	10	11	12
Emotional Stability	3	3	3	3
Initiative	4	4	3	3
Leadership	5	5	5	5
Social Attitude	4	4	5	5
Integrity	3	3	3	3

Questions—"Tired Ted: pass or fail?"

1. What kinds of information would have helped Mr. Thompson deal with Ted's boredom?
2. What is motivation and what causes it? How do rewards and punishment affect motivation? What relationships exist between motivation and learning?
3. If you could visit Ted's home, what kinds of relationships would you expect to find existing between Ted and his family?
4. What values does Ted seem to hold about education? Where is he likely to have obtained them? Why wasn't Ted a drop-out?
5. What kinds of pressures does the school seem to have placed on Ted? What effect does the threat of failure seem to have on Ted?
6. How does Ted probably perceive school? His teachers? Grades and graduation? Himself?
7. What effect would failure probably have on Ted? Is he likely to profit from retaking courses next year? What information might be helpful to Mr. Thompson before he decides whether he should fail Ted or not?
8. If Mr. Thompson and Mr. Brook pass Ted and he receives his diploma, what effect is it likely to have on Ted? What effect is it likely to have on other students who know him?
9. What effect does social promotion have on pupil achievement? On other aspects of pupil growth and development?
10. Will passing pupils like Ted cheapen the value of the high school diploma? What should Mr. Thompson do?

Providing
for individual
differences

Jackson Senior High School is located in a midwestern city of 75,000 population. Coal mining, industry, and agriculture all contribute to the city's
economy. The city's financial support of its schools is slightly below the
national average.

Jackson is a comprehensive high school with 1200 students in three
grades. Three buildings, which are basically square-shaped in design and
constructed of faded red brick, comprise its campus. The main building has
three floors of classrooms and is overcrowded with students since it was
originally built to hold a maximum of 1000.

The student body at Jackson is drawn from all the socio-economic strata
of the city, although middle-class students predominate. Seventy percent of
the members of each graduating class enter college.

Sam Goodman has taught social studies for five years. He is 26 years
old, married, and has two young children. His wife does not work.

Sam and about 40 other faculty members are attending the biweekly
faculty meeting in the school library. The furniture in the library is old but
well kept. The beige walls are covered with pictures, posters, announce-

ments, etc. Ray Carson, the principal, is handing out the schedule of classes for the second semester.

Mr. Carson: (As he passes out copies of the schedule) I'm very gratified that we didn't have to go on double sessions this semester. Believe me, it took a lot of figuring. As many of you know, I've had to ask some of you more experienced teachers to go that extra mile. Otherwise, we would have had to go on double sessions, for sure. This means that some of you old pros have had to give up your planning period. For that sacrifice we all thank you. (Mr. Carson smiles) The teachers' lounge won't be the same without you.

Most of the teachers smile and a few laugh audibly. Mr. Carson walks to a position in front of the librarian's desk and picks up some papers. He looks at the papers from time to time as he talks.

Mr. Carson: Let's talk about homeroom for a minute. Let me emphasize again that Tuesdays and Fridays are set aside for guidance. (With a grave expression on his face) Don't let students out of your homeroom on those days. Work with them on guidance activities. If you need materials beyond those that have been provided, please see Mr. Mallory, head of the Guidance and Counseling Center. Let me urge you to read the announcements carefully on Mondays. Make sure that all of the students are present and listening. (Pauses, looks down at the paper in his hand, and looks up again) (With emphasis) Now—on Wednesdays and Thursdays—and on those days only—students will be permitted to leave your homeroom for their clubs and activities. There will be no exception to this, this semester. Okay?

It is the first regular day of classes of the new semester. Sam is meeting with his homeroom and has finished reading the week's announcements.

At Jackson a teacher keeps the same homeroom for three years. Sam looks up at the students and smiles. He is seated at his desk.

Sam: Well, I guess we're all stuck with one another for another semester. In fact, unless I leave, we'll be together again next year when you all become dignified seniors. (Some of the students laugh) (The smile leaves Sam's face and he points his right index finger for emphasis) Mr. Carson has made it very clear that you will be here every day during homeroom period except Wednesdays and Thursdays. (Raises his voice) There will be absolutely no exceptions—not even for band members. (Several students laugh out loud and Sam smiles) Well, now that I've got that off my chest I guess we can work on guidance. Does anyone feel like he needs to be guided? (Again Sam smiles and several students laugh; one boy, George Ames, holds up his hand)

Sam: Yes, George.

George: Mr. Goodman, when will the magazine campaign begin this year?

Sam: (Gets up from his desk and paces) You would have to bring that up, George! (Sam smiles) I try not to think about it. I guess that it won't go away though. (Smile leaves Sam's face) It begins around the middle of

February, George. I'll bet you'll be the top salesman in the school again this year, too. (Sam walks back to his desk and sits down; he has a serious expression on his face) By the way, guys—the Executive Cabinet of the Tri-Torch Club will have to meet in here again on Thursdays. So, I'm going to have to ask those of you who stay here not to talk. (Several students groan audibly)

It is now the first period (8:40–9:35) of classes on the same day. Sam is meeting his world history class. Thirty-eight sophomores sit quietly as Sam sits on top of his desk and lectures.

Sam: I see that we have a few new people this semester. I hope that you all made it through the Middle Ages during the first semester because we are going to begin with the Renaissance in here. (One of the new students, Charles French, holds up his hand)

Sam: (Looking at Charles) Yes?

Charles: Mr. Goodman, how will you give us our grades in here?

Sam: As the old-timers in here can tell you, we'll have an objective-type of quiz, usually ten questions, over the text each Friday. We'll also have two or three examinations each six-weeks' grading period. They will be over the text, your notes on my lectures, and class discussions. Exams will all be announced in advanced—probably two will be objective and one will be essay. Okay?

Charles: Yes, thank you.

Sam: We may have some things like map work that will be graded also. (Sam gets down off the top of his desk and begins to pace as he lectures) Today, I'd like to begin by reviewing the factors that brought about the end of the Middle Ages.

Sam sits on top of his desk as he talks to 36 juniors in his seventh-period (2:40–3:35) United States history class. It is still the first day of classes.

Sam: I see that we have two new people this semester. Let me save time and tell you how your grades will be figured in here. We'll have a quiz every Friday over the text. We'll have two or three regular exams on the text and your notes. Be sure to take notes on class discussions. The tests will be mostly objective. (Sam smiles) I think that they are fairly difficult, too. You can ask some of the people who had me last semester—they have taken more of my tests than I have. (Several students laugh, others smile; a boy, Rick Ronson, holds up his hand)

Sam: Yes, Rick?

Rick: Will you meet with kids after school if they need help, like you did last semester?

Sam: I don't know, Rick. It's doubtful. With the schedule that I have this semester, I probably won't be able to. (Several students groan)

Sam: I'm sorry, guys. Tell your parents that we're so overcrowded here that the students are beginning to suffer. I hate it because I enjoyed those sessions as much as you guys did. (Smiling, Sam gets down off the top of his desk and begins to pace) Well, shall we begin to fight the Civil War? Bill, what were some of the causes of the Civil War?

The first day of classes is over and Sam sits in the principal's office. Both Sam and Mr. Carson have serious expressions on their faces as they talk. Mr. Carson sits behind his desk and Sam sits in a chair in front of the desk.

Sam: Ray, I've been here five years, and this is the worst schedule that I've ever had. I have four preparations—actually five, with my two United States history classes being so different, and 35 is my smallest class. I have 38 in world, 37 in one United States class and 36 in the other; I have 36 in civics and 35 in economics. That's 182 students, not counting the 35 in homeroom. (With emphasis) Now, Ray, that's a ridiculous load!

Mr. Carson: Sam, don't you think that I know that I'm asking a lot of you? Evans and Reardon are also stuck with around 180 kids.

Sam: Do they also have to give up their planning period to take a study hall? Do they also have to give up the last 15 minutes of their lunch hour once a week for hall duty? Do they have to sponsor a club that is *half* as big or *half* as active as Tri-Torch? I'll tell you, Ray—I won't be here next year if this keeps up!

Mr. Carson: (In a warm, pleading manner) Now, Sam, take it easy. I promise you that you won't have a schedule like this next year if I have anything to say about it. (Pauses) I'll level with you, Sam. I've put more on you than anyone this semester because you're the only one that I know can stand the pressure. I'll tell you something else, Sam. If I have anything to say about it, you'll be an administrator one of these days. (Sam calms down and begins to smile)

Sam: Well, I'll tell you, Ray. The thing that bothers me most is not being able to work with slow students after school.

Mr. Carson: You're working with a homebound student after school each day, aren't you?

Sam: Yes, I am. Frankly, Anita and I need the money.

Mr. Carson: (Nods his head and smiles) I know what you mean. (Becomes serious again) By the way, that reminds me. Coach Rawlings wants to ask you whether you want to sell basketball tickets at the home games again this year. That'll give you a little extra cash too.

Sam: I'll go over to the gym and see him before I go home.

Mr. Carson: By the way, Sam—I hate to ask you this, but the Tri-Torch Club will put on the Basketball Queen's Prom again this year, won't it?

Sam: (Frowning) Yes.

Mr. Carson: Sam, now either you or George Evans will have to be with them this year when they decorate the gym. (With emphasis) They cannot be left alone for a minute. We don't want any more incidents like the one last year.

Sam: (Still frowning) I agree—one of us will be there to supervise them.

Mr. Carson: (Smiling) Good—now do you feel better?

Sam: (Smiling) Not really—but I'll go along with you. (He adds with emphasis) But it *is* going to be a heck of a quarter.

Mr. Carson: It'll get better—but not right away. (They laugh as Mr. Carson walks with his arm around Sam's shoulders to the door)

Sam has just returned home after attending a class at a nearby teachers college where he is taking graduate courses toward his superintendent's license. His children are asleep and his wife, Anita, greets him as he comes in the livingroom hallway door of their middle-class home.

Anita: Hi, dear. How was class tonight? (Sam enters the livingroom and sits down in a chair)

Sam: I really don't know.

Anita: What do you mean?

Sam: I just heard Dr. Mason talk about one thing before I tuned him out.

Anita: (Intensely) Tuned him out? What did he say?

Sam: He talked about how important it is for a teacher to attempt to reach the individual needs of each child—providing for individual differences—you know.

Anita: Don't you agree with what he said?

Sam: Yes, I do. That's the problem.

Anita: What do you mean?

Sam: I tuned out the rest of his lecture and quit taking notes because I kept trying to think of ways of providing for individual differences in my own classes.

Anita: Did you think of any?

Sam: Nope. Like most profs, Mason lives in an ivory tower and doesn't practice what he preaches. I went up to him after class and showed him my schedule for this semester and asked him how I could provide for individual differences with a load like that.

Anita: What did he say?

Sam: Nothing practical. He just got me worked up for nothing. (Pauses) How can you provide for individual differences when you have a load like mine?

SCHEDULE OF CLASSES FOR SAM GOODMAN, ROOM 113
SECOND SEMESTER, JACKSON SENIOR HIGH SCHOOL

Period	Time	Subject	Grade	Enrollment
HR	8:05–8:35	Homeroom	11	35
1	8:40–9:35	World History	10	38
2	9:40–10:35	U. S. History	11	37
3	10:40–11:35	Civics	12	36
4	11:40–12:35	Lunch		
5	12:40–1:35	Economics	12	35
6	1:40–2:35	Study Hall		147
7	2:40–3:35	U. S. History	11	36

Questions—"Providing for individual differences"

1. Is it possible for the school to place so many demands on the teacher's time that it becomes impossible for him to individualize instruction or is it a question of motivation and/or lack of knowledge on the teacher's part? Is the failure to individualize instruction related to teacher frustration? How can the school help the teacher individualize instruction?

2. What are individual differences? What individual differences should the teacher concern himself with? How do individual differences relate to human growth and development? How are individual differences measured? What information does the high school teacher typically have available to him concerning differences existing between individual students? What are some other kinds of information that he could gather with a reasonable amount of effort?

3. What does it really mean to say that the teacher should attempt to "reach the whole child"? Is this a reasonable goal for the secondary teacher? What role should cocurricular activities play in this regard?

4. What are the human needs and how do they relate to motivation? How do individuals differ in terms of human needs? Is it really possible for a secondary teacher like Sam to assess the individual needs of each child in his classes and take them into consideration in his planning and actual instruction?

5. Are some teaching methods better suited to providing for individual differences? What would a curriculum be like that is built around individual differences? What are some of the teaching methods and curricula that teachers have developed in an attempt to take individual differences into consideration? Can teacher-pupil planning be utilized at the secondary level? What does it mean to individualize instruction?

6. Can the secondary teacher resolve the conflict of trying to teach both groups and individuals at the same time? How are individuals different when they are in a group than when they are alone? In what ways does a group like a class of students usually affect the behavior of individuals and vice versa?

7. What kinds of measurement and evaluation procedures should a teacher use in evaluating achievement if he attempts to individualize instruction? What problems are involved in evaluating a student on the basis of his individual growth (comparing him with his own past performance rather than comparing him to the group or a standard set by the teacher)? What role do rewards and punishment (such as grades) play in individualizing instruction?

8. Taking into consideration Sam's teaching load, how can he go about providing for individual differences?

9. Would the use of teacher aides help or hinder the teacher's efforts to individualize instruction? Would peer tutoring help? Do nongraded elementary and secondary schools do a better job of providing for individual differences than traditional schools?

Teacher to teacher

Mr. Williams, the principal of Edgemont Junior High School, anxiously looks at his desk calendar and mutters to himself, "New teacher orientation day. I hope I survive." Abruptly, he crushes his cigarette in the big oval ashtray and smiles broadly as Mrs. Sharp enters the room.

Ann Sharp has taught in Edgemont, a small town of 20,000 in a midwestern state, for five years. Mr. Williams is pleased to have Ann teaching at Edgemont Junior High; he knows that she is a good teacher. Each year several parents call him requesting that their son or daughter be placed in her social studies section. Students consistently describe her on evaluation forms as a fair, considerate teacher . . . a "cool head."

Bill: Good morning, Ann. It's good to see you this morning.

Ann: Good morning, Bill. I wanted to get a copy of the hall and lunch monitor assignments so I can let the new recruits know when they have duty.

Bill: (Pointing) You'll find them on the bottom shelf behind you—underneath the fire regulation pamphlets.

Ann: Got them. (She pauses) Say, can't you come in and say a few words to my group this morning?

Bill: No, I'll do my talking this afternoon when I speak to all the new teachers. I prefer to have a small group of new teachers meet with one experienced teacher before I speak to them. This way the new teachers have a chance to ask questions about things that really interest them. New teachers often feel foolish asking the principal about. . . .

Ann: (Interrupting) You mean they don't ask you about the things that really bother them?

Bill: (Nodding) Precisely.

Ann: Yes, I agree. I remember four years ago when you talked to us. I was afraid to ask you my real questions.

Bill: Such as?

Ann: Well, questions like: How much paper can I use? How does the duplicating machine work? How do I get movies and filmstrips? What are you going to look for when you come into my classroom? What do you think a good teacher is?

Bill: Good, you get the idea. I want them to get answers for those questions.

Ann: Can you tell me anything about the three new social studies teachers that I will be working with in orientation? Last night I examined their placement folders and the girls all looked like the same person. You know, it's hard to tell about a new teacher until you actually teach her. They all had good marks in school and all had A's in student teaching and their letters of recommendation read like a carbon copy.

Bill: I know. (He adds wryly) Almost all the applicants have earned A's in student teaching. Cooperating teachers become so ego-involved with their student teachers that they feel if a girl receives a B or a C it is a sign of their failure as a cooperating teacher. (In exasperation) These girls are graded artificially high and there is no way to tell high-potential teachers from low-potential teachers.

Ann: Then you don't remember anything about the girls?

Bill: Let's see. No, nothing in particular—except, perhaps, Cynthia Clove. During the interview she seemed to put on airs; but that was probably just me.

Ann: (With a puzzled look) What do you mean, put on airs?

Bill: Well, she seemed afraid to talk about herself or what she felt. She constantly referred to what one of her professors had said about ability grouping or what some textbook said about retaining students. She never voiced her opinion. It was almost as if she didn't have opinions of her own. It was like she was role playing—like she was playing the role of a concerned teacher. But as I said, it was probably just me or a bad day for her. Say, you better get going. It's time to meet the troops. (Smiling) Tell it like it is!

Ann: See you later.

Ann finishes her 30-minute orientation speech and is greeted by three enthusiastic, almost indistinguishable voices (June Morton, Cynthia Clove, and Betty Jordon, three recent graduates from the state university).

Cynthia: Ann, you've really made us feel welcome!

June: Thanks for letting us know what is expected here. I'm glad you gave us both the good news and the mundane.

Betty: Ann, if the other teachers are as frank and helpful as you are, this is going to be a good school for me.

Ann: (Smiling) Thanks for your nice comments. I'm glad we can work together. We've gone over the stuff I wanted to talk about. What questions do you have? (Earnestly) Anything goes. (The girls lower their heads, shuffle their feet, and furiously scribble on their note pads) Take a minute or two and write down your questions and then we'll read them all. Maybe two or three can be answered at one time. (After a two-minute pause) Okay—read your questions and I'll take notes.

Cynthia: (Hesitantly) If you think students are cheating, how do you handle it?

June: Why do students cheat?

Betty: (With eager anticipation) What enrichment materials can we use with our fast students?

Cynthia: How do you know if the children really like you? (Angrily) When children are truant, whom do we call?

Betty: What's a good way to start off class on the first day to get a serious but relaxed atmosphere?

Cynthia: How do you keep from getting bored in the classroom, doing the same thing every day?

June: How can we involve parents in the school program?

Betty: How closely do we have to follow the curriculum guide?

Cynthia: When the curriculum supervisor enters the classroom, what will she want to see?

Ann: Well, that's a good list of questions. Let's start with the first two. Betty and Cynthia were concerned about student cheating. . . .

Cynthia: (Interrupting) I'm not really concerned. I'm just interested in getting more effective techniques. In college we were taught to reinforce behaviors incompatible with those you want to decrease. . . .

That afternoon in the principal's office, Bill Williams and Ann Sharp review the orientation program.

Bill: (Warmly) Ann, I was really pleased with the orientation program this afternoon. I felt like I was talking with, not to, the new teachers.

Ann: You did a good job. I think the teachers respect you and are satisfied to be working with you.

Bill: Well, if I did a good job it was because you and the three other orientation teachers did some good spade work in the morning session. How did it go?

Ann: It went very well. They really responded to my opening remarks and June and Betty became involved in the question and answer period.

Bill: What about Cynthia?

Ann: (Frowning) I'm worried about Cynthia. I was bothered by Cynthia's reaction during the discussion. She would half-listen to me or one of the other girls respond to her question; then she would quickly answer her own question, insisting that the question was not of real concern to her but just something she wanted to toss out so she could get someone else's opinion. She kept a little distance between herself and the discussion. She seemed afraid to enter the conversation. (With concern) Bill, I hope your comments didn't bias me but I think she's going to have problems in the classroom. She's concerned, perhaps worried, about teaching but unable to admit it and to discuss her reservations.

One month later, the curriculum supervisor (making her first visit to Cynthia's room) enters the room and takes a seat in the back of the room as Cynthia begins her presentation.

Cynthia: Now I want you to read Chapter 15 by yourself without any noise or moving around. You have 20 minutes to read pages 110 to 125 about how a bill becomes a law. When you finish, we can talk about it.

Four students approach the desk. Two need to go to the rest room and the other two left their books in their lockers. She gives all of them permission to leave. They depart noisily from the room. Randy, a student in the middle of the room, waves his hand furiously until Cynthia spots him.

Cynthia: (Harshly) Well, Randy, what do you want?
Randy: Mrs. Clove, I read this last night.
Cynthia: Well, read it again or just relax. Keep quiet and let the other students work.

Randy frowns, lowers his head, and eventually turns to look out the window. Finally he begins to write his initials on the desk. Moments later, Cynthia hurriedly approaches his desk.

Cynthia: Randy, what are you doing?
Randy: Nothing. I didn't have anything to do and. . . .
Cynthia: (Said with exasperation) You never have anything to do, do you? Can't you sit in a seat for 10 minutes and not bother anyone? Watch the clock for ten minutes!

Randy watches the clock for 10 minutes and then, unnoticed by Cynthia, finishes writing his initials on the desk. Two students carefully observe Randy as he places the finishing touches on the desk. Both then begin scribbling on their desks with a pencil. Cynthia looks up as the two students finally return from the rest room. She notices that it took them 15 minutes but she doesn't say anything. She looks at the class and notices several students with their heads on their desks.

Cynthia: Well, now that we've finished reading, let's see what we know. . . .
Class: (In chorus) We need more time! Not yet!
Bill: (A large student sitting in the rear of the room—shouting out) Hey, I know. Let's pass a law. We can set up committees and do the whole bit.
Cynthia: Perhaps we can do that next week, but first we'd better learn how to pass laws. Besides, we're already two units behind in the book. Now, who can tell me how a bill gets on the calendar? Ruth, (One of her best students, who is sitting in the front row) can you answer that?

Cynthia thumbs to the answer section in the teacher edition and looks for her next question as she half listens to Ruth's answer. When Ruth finishes, Cynthia immediately looks at Jim.

Cynthia: Jim, can you tell me. . . .

Later that evening at home Cynthia washes dishes and her husband, Tom, reads the sports news at the kitchen table.

Cynthia: (Angrily) Tom, I have never been so humiliated in all my life. Doesn't that supervisor know I've only been teaching four weeks. What can you expect from kids like these anyway? They don't care about school or anything else for that matter. I think the principal gave me the hardest kids in school to teach.
Tom: Well, hon, what did the supervisor criticize? What did she say?
Cynthia: Oh, she criticized everything.
Tom: Like what?
Cynthia: I can't remember specifics. She, ah . . . ah. . . . I don't know. Sometimes I don't think I want to be a teacher.

Two days later in the principal's office, Bill Williams and Ann Sharp talk about Cynthia's teaching effectiveness.

Bill: Now that you have read the curriculum supervisor's detailed account of what went on in Cynthia's room during her visit, what do you think?
Ann: It matches pretty well with my impression. Cynthia has never been in my room to see me so we haven't had time to really talk at length. However, her room is directly across the hall from mine and I stop in almost every morning to exchange a few words. Each morning I get the same story: "Everything's fine, no problems at all!" (Firmly) However, everything's not fine. During her last two weeks I have been interrupted by noise and confusion coming from her room. The only day in the last few days that her kids have been quiet was when the curriculum supervisor visited her room. (She adds) Even with her door closed, you can hear everything quite clearly. It's getting difficult for me to control my class, and other teachers in our wing have started to complain.
Bill: I have had a couple of calls from parents saying that Cynthia has been extremely critical of their child, but I didn't pay much attention to their reports until I received the supervisor's report and now you tell me. . . .
Ann: (Interrupting) I'm sorry, I should have mentioned it to you but it's only been really bad for the last five or six days. I hoped that she would come and talk to me. I thought that would be better; but obviously she's not going to come to me. Bill, as her orientation teacher, I feel that I should be the one to talk with her. But how can I help her to examine the situation openly and undefensively?

Questions—"Teacher to teacher"

1. Should Ann be the one to talk to Cynthia, or should the principal or curriculum supervisor talk to her? Should Ann have tried to help Cynthia without talking to the principal first? Under what circumstances should a teacher approach another teacher to question his classroom instructional activities and his general effectiveness?

2. What can Ann do to increase the possibilities for having an open and productive discussion of Cynthia's teaching? What will determine whether Cynthia will be threatened by what Ann has to say or not? How do threat and anxiety affect learning? What relationships exist between threat and the self-concept?

3. If Cynthia says to Ann, "What can you expect from children like these," how can Ann respond in a nonthreatening way?

4. Do the relationships existing between threat and learning also apply to children? To relations with parents?

5. What are defense mechanisms and what purpose do they serve? How do you deal with defensive behavior?

6. How can Ann help Cynthia to remember the specifics of her classroom behavior? What is systematic observation of teacher behavior and how can it be used? What specific behaviors did Cynthia engage in that you would point out to her? Why?

7. The new teachers asked several questions during orientation day. Do these questions provide clues as to what the young teachers were *really* concerned about? What concerns do new teachers have? Do their concerns differ from those of experienced teachers?

Portrait
of a concerned
parent

Jim Williams turned his new, light-blue Buick into the driveway and care-fully headed the car up the winding pavement toward his five-bedroom brick house. Jim looked at the house, which sits some 250 feet from the street and is heavily surrounded by trees and shrubs, and could only see its diffuse outline through the heavy thicket. He carefully noticed the large rose bushes spaced at four-foot intervals as he wound his way up the drive.

Jim is a Senior Vice-president at a prominent local bank. He has resided in this southeastern city of over 200,000 for 15 years. He parked the car beside his wife's Lincoln, entered the side door of the house, walked to his study, and deposited his briefcase on the large walnut desk. He then walked to the spacious, comfortable-looking family room and found Helen, his at-tractive wife, reading the evening newspaper. She smiled warmly as he en-tered the room and beamed radiantly when he kissed her lightly on the cheek.

Mr. Williams: Hi, hon. How's Ruth's cold?

Ruth, their 5-year-old daughter, is the younger of their two children.

Mrs. Williams: This morning the doctor described her as being "fit as a fiddle" and told her to go ahead and play, but not to over-do it. She's outside in the back yard making up for the four days she had to stay inside.

Mr. Williams: That's good news! Let's take the family up to the lake this weekend for skiing and a picnic. Say, where's Linda?

Mrs. Williams: (Said with evident concern) Jim, she's outside with Ruth, and while she is I want to talk to you about her sex education program.

Mr. Williams: (His face reddens) Linda's sex education program? You mean you want *me* to talk with her about sex?

Mrs. Williams: (Obviously amused) No, silly! I'm talking about the sex education program at school. I'm sure the teacher is well qualified and the materials must have been approved by the school board, but I'm still uneasy.

Mr. Williams: Oh, honey, you're terrific—always the conscientious mother. You're just making a problem in your mind.

Mrs. Williams: (With irritation) It's not just me. Some of the other mothers have also raised an eyebrow or two.

Mr. Williams: Okay, then let's talk. You won't be happy until we do. How has this school sex thing affected Linda?

Mrs. Williams: She's started to read several paperbacks. Several of them are innocent books about baby birth and child care. But this afternon I was reading through her health-sex education notebook and I found notes about various birth contraceptives. They must be lecturing on this in school. I don't think a 14-year-old girl should be reading birth control literature, do you?

Mr. Williams: I don't know. I really would have to know more about how it's presented in class. However, if a junior high school teacher is talking about contraceptives in a class, he had better be presenting the information very carefully and intelligently. I think. . . .

Mrs. Williams: (Breaking in anxiously) You know that she is also reading *Peyton Place* and *Lady Chatterly's Lover*. Could these books be school assignments?

Mr. Williams: (With finality) No, I am sure that they aren't class books, but perhaps they are talking about these books in class and that stimulated her interest to buy them. You know Linda, she's naturally curious. If I keep listening to you, I am going to become suspicious of the program. Who is her health teacher?

Mrs. Williams: Jean Johnson. She's a young, pretty thing. This is her third or fourth year at junior high.

That evening at the end of dinner the family lingers discussing Linda's school work.

Mr. Williams: It sounds like Mr. Clinton, your algebra teacher, is a good teacher. Those problem exercises must have taken him hours to construct.

Linda: Yeah, he's a good teacher and a real charmer. He's really quite a man. (Mr. and Mrs. Williams exchange worried glances)

Mrs. Williams: What do you mean, "quite a man"?

Linda: (Said enthusiastically and with a raised eyebrow) Oh, you know, he's been around.

Mr. Williams: (Face reddens and anger in his voice) Does he flirt with you girls?

Linda: Oh, Daddy, you're adorable! (She reaches over and hugs him) No, he doesn't flirt with the girls. He's pure and proper; he's above us girls.

Mr. Williams: Say, I don't want to sound like the conservative old man that I am, but I am curious about the sex education course you have at school. What do you talk about in the course?

Linda: Oh, Daddy, I didn't think you would be a parent to complain. Mrs. Johnson said some of the parents might be a little sensitive but I never thought. . . .

Mr. Williams: (His voice becoming louder) Listen, I just want to know what's going on. I'm curious. You can tell Mrs. Johnson that if she would communicate with parents they might not feel sensitive.

Mrs. Williams: Yes, I don't think it was wise for Mrs. Johnson to suggest to the class that parents. . . .

Linda: (Breaking in) Mother, good grief—don't get carried away. Dad made the point. I hear what you're both saying. The course as you call it isn't even a course—in health class we are talking about sex education topics for six weeks.

Mrs. Williams: (Cynically) Such as?

Linda: Well, the last few periods we had been talking about the population explosion and the zero population growth advocates. Then we started to talk about how the poor contribute disproportionately to the population because many are not educated about birth control methods. So we discussed the advisability of giving them information that they could apply.

Mrs. Williams: So you study methods of birth control, like the pill.

Linda: Sure, the pill, diaphragms, foam, rhythm, etc. You name it and we have studied it. Those discussions bored me. (Mr. and Mrs. Williams exchange relieved glances) But today we started a discussion that is really exciting. We had talked about female power in government class and when we went to health class several of us were still talking about it. So Debbie Green, I think it was Debbie, got the class off to a roaring start by asking Mrs. Johnson if sex was really good for women or if it was just another way in which men used women. We had a good discussion and she suggested some library references for us to consult if we want to at the public library.

Mr. Williams: What books were recommended?

Linda: Oh, I can't remember. I think *Sex and the Single Girl* or something like that was mentioned.

Mrs. Williams: Did the teacher suggest the book or did one of the girls?

Linda: I can't remember. But I can tell you that Mrs. Johnson is really with it. She's a good teacher and her course is important to me.

That same evening as Mrs. Johnson is getting ready for bed, the telephone rings.

Mr. Williams: Mrs. Johnson, this is Mr. Williams, Linda's father.

Mrs. Johnson: Yes, hello, Mr. Williams. What can I do for you?

Mr. Williams: I want to see you as soon as possible and discuss your health class.

Mrs. Johnson: (With a slight tremor in her voice) Why, has something offended you or has Linda. . . .

Mr. Williams: No, Linda is fine. She likes you and the course. But I want to find out more about the course. I want to know about *your* reading materials and what your concrete goals are for this course. To be perfectly frank, I am a bit concerned about the course; but I have only heard Linda's vague description. I haven't seen any description of this program in the paper and it hasn't been discussed at PTA. I am very interested in seeing you and finding out what's going on. Mrs. Johnson, I hope it is a good course, but I don't think you should be recommending books like *Sex and the Single Girl* to your students and . . . well, let's wait and talk about it tomorrow.

Quesitons—"Portrait of a concerned parent"

1. Are schools any better prepared to handle sex education than are parents? Should schools obtain parental approval before allowing students to enroll in sex education training programs? Should schools emphasize physical sex, psycho-affectional sex, or both?
2. Some adolescents suggest that adults are unwilling to discuss sex on a realistic and explicit level. How explicit should a sex education program be? What topics should be included? Specifically, what books would you include in a sex education program for young adolescents?
3. Why do you suppose that Linda says the sex education program is important to her? In what ways might a sex education program help students in their quest for ego identity and executive independence?
4. What social class differences exist with respect to how adolescents deal with their sex drives? In what ways can schools help adolescents understand their newly acquired sexuality?
5. Is Mr. Williams an interfering parent? What role should such organizations as the PTA play in fostering home-school communication?
6. How should a school develop its sex education program so as to obtain maximal community understanding and support?
7. What general skills are necessary for a good teacher-parent conference? How should Mrs. Johnson proceed in this particular conference?

To strike
or not to strike

Central High is a comprehensive high school located in a medium-sized city in a southern state. White students outnumber black students three to one. Joe Collins is a 27-year-old English teacher and is an assistant football and basketball coach. He has four years' teaching experience.

The teachers' lounge at Central High, like the rest of the school building, is equipped with old furniture that is kept in good repair. The chairs are covered with different colored materials with green dominating. Two coffee tables of different colored woods are covered with educational magazines and journals, and a silver 30-cup coffee urn sits on a table along with coffee supplies.

Six teachers (four male teachers, including the head football coach, and two female teachers) are seated in the lounge as Joe enters.

Coach Wilson: Hey, Joe. What did you think about what the board did to us last night?

The other teachers stop talking and listen intently for Joe's response as he walks to the coffee urn to get a cup of coffee.

Joe: I didn't think much of it, to say the least. Did you go to the meeting?
Coach Wi'son: All of us were there except Millie and Ann.

Ann: I had to grade a mess of compositions last night and Millie had no way to get there.

George: I'm sorry, Millie, I could have picked you up if I'd known that you didn't have a ride.

Millie: That's okay. I don't think that I would have enjoyed myself anyhow.

Coach Wilson: (Laughing) Boy, that's for sure. (Pause—then a frown) You know what bugged me though? When Kramer (60-year-old male math teacher) gets up and thanks the gentlemen of the board for the careful consideration that they gave the matter before deciding that they could not ask the county tax board to increase taxes. The dumb-dumb actually thanked them for not giving us any salary increases next year! (He shakes his head)

Joe: He also thanked them for not building any new buildings or even adding new rooms to old buildings.

George: I liked Samuels' (President of the school board) comment when he was asked by Ray (shop teacher) if he knew that Central was designed for 1000 students but has over 1600 in it.

Coach Wilson: Wasn't that something, the slob. I wish he had that clothing store of his stuck up his tail! (Looks at Millie and Ann) You'll have to excuse me today, girls. (Looks back to men) But it makes me so damn mad to think of him giving out with that business about not asking the taxpayers to "bear more of an already unbearable burden." (Coach Wilson pounds the arm of his chair with a vigorous gesture)

Joe: I can't wait until the meeting tomorrow night. We have put up with this kind of crap from the board for the last ten years. (Joe gets up and paces the floor) We have always solved the board's problems for them, like sticking Millie (Joe points toward Millie) in that broom closet with 40 kids. The problems always get solved by us so the board figures that will continue to happen. But all good things have to come to an end and I have a feeling that this will be the straw that breaks the camel's back. The teachers won't stand for another year without a raise. (Joe slams his coffee cup down on the table)

Coach Wilson: Do you really think that the board is afraid of the ATO? You think that the teachers really have guts enough to do anything other than protest? Remember, Kramer is the President!

The regular monthly meeting of the local branch of the American Teachers Organization is underway in the Central High School auditorium. Mr. Kramer presides on the stage at one end of the auditorium while over 1000 teachers are seated in seats that are bolted to the floor.

Mr. Kramer: It is the opinion of the President that the ayes have it. The dues of each member will be increased $2.00 to provide us with a permanent flower fund. Is there any other new business? (Looks at Joe who is waving his hand) Yes—Joe Collins.

Joe: Mr. President, I am deeply distressed that this meeting is almost over and absolutely no mention has been made of the action taken by the school board yesterday. I. . . .

Mr. Kramer: (Angrily) Mr. Collins, you are out of order. This is not the time or place. . . .

Coach Wilson: What the hell do you mean he is out of order! You recognized him, so according to the rules of order he still has the floor. If you don't let him finish, I'm going to walk out of here right now and I bet a lot of people go with me! (About half the teachers loudly shout their support of Coach Wilson)

Mr. Kramer: (Raps gavel vigorously for order) Let's have some order! (Voice grows more strident) Let's have order! Act like teachers instead of a mob!

Voice from rear: Quit acting like a dictator, Kramer, and let Joe speak! (Other voices pick up the chant, "Let Joe speak!") If that's the way that you all feel, I am resigning as President right now. (He turns to Coach Wilson and says bitterly) You seem to want to run this meeting, Coach Wilson, so why don't you take over?

Mr. Kramer angrily stuffs his notes into a folder and walks out of the auditorium. He is followed by his officers and about 25 other teachers. Coach Wilson steps up on the stage.

Coach Wilson: I have no desire to take over this meeting. But I'll tell you one thing, friends, if we don't take some action right now to deal with the school board, the kids of this country are going to end up getting a tenth-rate education instead of a second-rate one. Personally, I've had it and I'm ready to take action. (The crowd yells support) I've given this matter a lot of thought. I think that we should elect five teachers to represent all of us and let them go tell the school board how we feel.

Teacher #1: It certainly never hurts to try to talk reasonably to the board, but I want to go on record as saying that I don't think that we should try to stir things up at this time. We don't even have a President to accept your motion.

Teacher #2: Mr. Kramer and all the rest of the officers resigned, didn't they? (Turns to Teacher #3) Jake, as last year's President, why don't you take temporary charge of the meeting until we can nominate new officers and act on Coach Wilson's motion? (Turns toward audience) I nominate Coach Wilson for President. (Crowd approves with less enthusiasm than before)

It is the day after Coach Wilson and four teachers have met with the school board. Ten teachers and Coach Wilson are in the teachers' lounge.

Coach Wilson: (Pacing) So the five of us had no sooner sat down and Samuels says, "I hear that you are the new ATO President, Coach Wilson. How many of the county teachers do you five gentlemen represent?" (Hits palm with fist) I could have hit him.

George: What got me was when we presented the comparison data on teachers' salaries and on the money being spent on buildings and instructional equipment. I pointed out that we ranked next to last in everything and Walters (a school board member) says, "Do we have to keep up with the Joneses?"

Coach Wilson: Then Farmer (another board member) says, (Mimicking) "I want to say, Coach Wilson, that I personally am very disappointed with the unprofessional behavior of the ATO. Teachers always want more money, but in the past the ATO has always dealt with the board in a very professional way. The only reason that I came to this so-called meeting tonight was to tell you that." Then they decided that since we really didn't have any new business, the meeting was adjourned. (Throws up his arms in exasperation)

Joe: (With concern) What are we going to do, Frank?

Coach Wilson: I don't know for sure, Joe. We should all walk out. I have called an emergency ATO meeting for Friday at the old Roxy Theatre. We'll see what happens.

Five-hundred teachers nearly fill all of the seats in an old movie theatre. Coach Wilson and four ATO officers are on the stage of the theatre. The four officers are seated while Coach Wilson stands and talks to the audience through a microphone that buzzes from time to time.

Coach Wilson: Some people say that we are public servants, not professionals, and put us in the same group as garbagemen, firemen, and policemen. They say that we are not allowed to strike. Others say that we are professionals and are like doctors. They also say that we should not strike since doctors don't. (Shouting) Well, are we or aren't we professionals?

Crowd: (Roars) Yes!

Coach Wilson: I don't believe that a school board that has threatened to send the names of any teachers who strike to the draft board, as ours did just last night, considers us to be professionals. (Hits podium with fist. The crowd murmurs) We are not in a private, fee-taking position like doctors. In fact, the doctors fear socialized medicine because they don't want to be in the same fix that we're in. We have socialized education already. In many ways we are more like labor in the typical labor-management situation in industry. Unlike labor, which has strong unions, nobody listens to us or cares what we have to say. (Raises his voice) I say that the product that we produce—educated citizens—is more important than most products industry produces. Yet one member of our school board said recently that if the superintendent of schools would shape up the teachers of this school system the way that he shapes up the workers in his business, all our educational problems would disappear. (Pauses, shaking his head) I'm afraid, my fellow teachers, that the only way we can fight the powers that would rather see our children get a tenth-rate education than raise taxes is to use power ourselves. (He speaks slowly and with emphasis) Therefore, as your ATO President and after much consultation with your executive committee, I recommend to you that we not strike, but that we walk out. I suggest that we all sign the mimeographed resignation forms that are now being passed out. (Points toward men passing out forms) After you have signed, knowing full well that if we lose this fight you have not only lost your job but will probably even have to leave this state to find employment (Pauses), give them to your building representatives. We will present all of them to the school board at once if the board refuses to change its stand. The floor is now open for questions or business.

Six teachers are in the teachers' lounge: Ann, the English teacher; Millie, a social studies teacher; George, a social studies teacher; Coach Barber, the basketball coach; Ray, the chemistry teacher; and Joe.

Coach Barber: Only half of the teachers turned out for the meeting and you know that all of them are not going to sign resignation slips. (Raises his voice) I figure that if the community, the parents, and over half the teachers don't give a crap, why should I be a martyr and lay my job on the line for nothing! Already the Quarterback Club has threatened to withdraw its support of the football team if Coach Wilson turns in the resignations to the board.

Ray: (Flatly) I hate to disagree with you guys, but I'm old-fashioned: A contract is a contract.

Coach Barber: (Speaks with controlled anger) Is it still a contract even if the board breaks it first? Of course the contract in this system is very vague as far as teaching conditions are concerned. The only place that it is specific is where it favors the board.

Ray: I don't know about that, but I don't think that you can beat city hall—especially when the superintendent always does what the board tells him. He'd never fight them on our behalf. I figure that if I strike, the only thing that I'm going to gain is to lose my job, and my car-wash business will probably go broke to boot.

Ann: I agree with you, Ray. A contract is a contract. With Gary (Ann's husband) in graduate school, I couldn't quit if I wanted to.

Millie: I knew that I wouldn't make all the money in the world when I became a teacher. If I didn't love to teach I would have gotten out a long time ago. I think that we all knew what we were getting into.

George: (Sharply) I guess I'd feel like you do too, Millie, if I were a woman and was married to a dentist who has a successful practice. (Millie's face flushes and she gets up and leaves)

Ann: (Sharply) That's pretty dirty, George, especially when the only thing that you guys are really striking for is more money!

Joe: That's not true, Ann, but if you believe that, then I am sure that most of the townspeople will. (Ann leaves)

Coach Barber: Watch what will happen. The men will walk out and 90 percent of the women won't. Yet, they'll want all the benefits that we'll gain if we win. I'll bet you that we won't close one-fourth of the elementary schools.

Joe Collins sits alone in his classroom at his desk. He stares at a resignation form that he holds in his hand. Coach Wilson walks by the open door, stops, watches Joe for a second, and walks into the room. Joe sees him but says nothing as the Coach sits down in a chair next to the desk.

Coach Wilson: I'll give you ten-to-one odds that I can guess what you're thinking about.

Joe: Believe it or not, I was thinking about Hamlet.

Coach Wilson: (Laughs) You're kidding! At a time like this!

Joe: Actually, I was killing two birds with one stone. My thoughts went like this. (Mimics Hamlet) To strike or not to strike; that is the question. Should I suffer the slings and arrows of inadequate facilities, personnel, space, and salary, not to mention too damn many students, or should I put my job, my family, and my bank account on the line by signing this paper? Shakespeare should have had such a problem! (Pauses, stands up, and paces) It could really be tough getting a job in another state even though the national ATO has agreed to help. And what about the students? Is it really fair to make this year's kids suffer for the sake of those in the future—especially when we may lose? If the schools fail to close, what kind of incompetents will the board put in the classrooms with the kids while we're striking? Who will take over my classes if I sign? (Shakes his head) Man, these are really the times that try men's souls. (Sits back down)

Coach Wilson: That's for sure, Joe, and you only know the half of it. I'm in a spot where I couldn't back down now even if I wanted to. I don't really have a decision to make anymore. (Voice breaks slightly) I want you to know, Joe, that I won't hold it against you if you decide not to strike.

Joe: Thanks, Frank. You'll never know how much I admire you for the stand that you've taken on this thing. (Stands up) I've got to go home now and talk things over with my family. We've got a decision to make tonight.

Questions—"To strike or not to strike"

1. What is a professional? To what extent is the teacher a professional? Does the teacher's role as a worker compare more closely to that of a doctor or to that of a skilled worker in industry? Is the role of the school administrator (such as the principal or superintendent) different from that of the teacher? Do the teachers in this problem situation see themselves as professionals?
2. What is a role in society? What is status and what are norms? What is the role of the teacher in our society? How much status does society ascribe to the teacher's role and why? Historically, how has the teacher's role evolved in our society? Does the role of the elementary teacher differ from that of the secondary teacher? Do they both differ from the college professor? To what extent does the community influence the teacher's role? How do the teachers in this problem situation tend to view their role as a teacher?
3. What is power? Who holds power in a school system? Do school systems differ with respect to the relative amounts of power held by the school board, the school administration, and the teachers? Should teachers obtain more power? Does the doctor have more power than the teacher? Why or why not? How do the teachers in this problem situation seem to feel about the above questions?
4. How does the school system discipline the behavior of a teacher who rocks the boat? How are rewards and punishment related to the exercise of power? What are the rewards of teaching? How are teachers punished? Is there a difference between internal and external rewards and punishment? What rewards and punishments seem to be operating in the cases of Joe and Coach Wilson?
5. What are social institutions and how do they affect one another? What are the functions of the educational institution in our society? How is a school like and different from a factory? What is the school's product? What is learning? Does learning differ from achievement? What nonacademic activities does a school engage in? Should the school really be responsible for the whole child? What is a school's curriculum?
6. Do teachers as a professional group seem to have a common set of needs that motivate their behavior? What are frustration and conflict? What is teacher morale? Is teacher frustration related to: (A) the teacher's classroom behavior; (B) teaching methods; (C) the curriculum; (D) teacher beliefs; (E) the way that the teacher sees himself? What needs, frustrations, and conflicts seem to be operating in this problem situation?
7. To what extent do variables outside the classroom affect what goes on inside? What are some of the variables that affect teacher behavior and pupil achievement, creativity, and learning? What variables seem to be operating in this situation?
8. From what social class do most teachers come? What values are characteristic of this social class? Do the teacher's sex and race affect the values that he holds? What values do Joe and Coach Wilson seem to hold? How do they differ from those held by others, especially the members of the school board?
9. What is communication and what variables affect it? What relationships exist between the way two different people view the world and their ability to communicate? How do people develop different perceptions of the world and how do such perceptions change? How does information that threatens the self usually affect perceptions and communication? Under what conditions is effective communication likely to take place between two people? Between one group and another group? How do the above relate to this case?
10. What is propaganda? What are competition and conflict as they relate to groups?

What variables foster communication between groups during times of conflict? What is objectivity and how can conflicting groups be persuaded to be objective and rational when negotiating? What is negotiation? What are mediation and arbitration? What is collective bargaining? Do any of the above seem to apply to this case?

11. Should Joe attempt to obtain any more information about the situation before he makes a decision? What can he, as an individual, actually do about the situation at this point in its development? Could he have done anything earlier? What decision should Joe make?

Bibliography

The following bibliography should prove useful in analyzing problem situations from the standpoint of psychological theory. Both primary and secondary sources are included and are organized under the headings of types of psychological theories or under the names of psychological theorists.

Relationship between educational psychology and teaching

Aspy, D. N. "Educational Psychology: Challenged or Challenging?" *Journal of Teacher Education,* 21 (1970): 5–13.

Blair, G. M.; Jones, R. S.; and Simpson, R. H. *Educational Psychology.* 3rd ed. New York: Macmillan, 1968.

Brown, B. B. *The Experimental Mind in Education.* New York: Harper & Row, 1968.

Chaplin, J. P., and Krawiec, T. S. *Systems and Theories of Psychology.* 2nd ed. New York: Holt, Rinehart & Winston, 1968.

Clayton, T. E. *Teaching and Learning: A Psychological Perspective.* Englewood Cliffs, N.J.: Prentice-Hall, 1965.

Coladarci, A. P. "The Teacher as Hypothesis Maker." *California Journal of Instructional Improvement,* 2 (1959): 3–6.

Gordon, I. J. *Criteria for Theories of Instruction.* Washington, D.C.: Association for Supervision and Curriculum Development, National Education Association, 1968.

Jackson, P. W. *Life in Classrooms.* New York: Holt, Rinehart & Winston, 1968.

Koch, S. *Psychology: A Study of a Science.* New York: McGraw-Hill, 1959.

Koch, S. "Psychology Cannot Be a Coherent Science." *Psychology Today*, 3 (September, 1969): 14+.

Marx, M. H. *Theories in Contemporary Psychology*. New York: Macmillan, 1963.

Marx, M. H., and Hillis, W. *Systems and Theories in Psychology*. New York: McGraw-Hill, 1963.

McDonald, F. J. *Educational Psychology*. 2nd ed. Belmont, Calif.: Wadsworth, 1965.

Peddiwell, J. A. *The Saber-tooth Curriculum*. New York: McGraw-Hill, 1939.

Perkins, H. V. *Human Development and Learning*. Belmont, Calif.: Wadsworth, 1969.

Snyder, H. I. *Contemporary Educational Psychology: Some Models Applied to the School Setting*. New York: Wiley, 1968.

Watson, G. "What Psychology Can We Feel Sure About?" In *Human Dynamics in Psychology and Education*, edited by D. E. Hamachek. Boston: Allyn & Bacon, 1968.

Watson, R. "A Brief History of Educational Psychology." In *Readings in Educational Psychology*, edited by H. C. Lindgren. New York: Wiley, 1968.

Wolman, B. B. *Contemporary Theories and Systems in Psychology*. New York: Harper & Row, 1960.

Motivational theory

Cofer, C. N., and Appley, M. H. *Motivation: Theory and Research*. New York: Wiley, 1964.

Dinkmeyer, D., and Dreikurs, R. *Encouraging Children to Learn: The Encouragement Process*. Englewood Cliffs, N.J.: Prentice-Hall, 1963.

Dollard, J., et al. *Frustration and Aggression*. New Haven: Yale University Press, 1939.

Harlow, H. "Mice, Monkeys, Men and Motives." *Psychological Review*, 60 (1953): 23–32.

Harlow, H. "The Nature of Love," *American Psychologist*, 13 (1958): 673–685.

Holt, J. *How Children Learn*. New York: Pitman, 1967.

Madsen, K. B. *Theories of Motivation*. rev. ed. Warren, Ohio: Kent State University Press, 1969.

Marx, M. H., and Tombaugh, T. N. *Motivation: Psychological Principles and Educational Implications*. San Francisco: Chandler, 1967.

McClelland, D. C. *Studies in Motivation*. New York: Appleton-Century-Crofts, 1955.

Murray, H. A. *Explorations in Personality*. New York: Oxford University Press, 1938.

Maslow

Maslow, A. H. "A Theory of Human Motivation." *Psychological Review*, 50 (1943): 370–396.

Maslow, A. H. "Higher and Lower Needs." *Journal of Psychology*, 25 (1948): 433–436.

Maslow, A. H. *Motivation and Personality*. New York: Harper & Row, 1954.

Maslow, A. H. "Self-Actualizing People: A Study of Psychological Health." In *Values in Personality Research*, edited by W. Wolff, Symposium No. 1. New York: Grune & Stratton, 1950.

Maslow, A. H. *Toward a Psychology of Being*. 2nd ed. Princeton, N.J.: Van Nostrand, 1968.

Perceptual psychology

Coopersmith, S. *The Antecedents of Self-esteem*. San Francisco: Freeman, 1967.
Hamachek, D. E., ed. *The Self: In Growth, Teaching and Learning*. Englewood Cliffs, N.J.: Prentice-Hall, 1965.
Jersild, A. T. *In Search of Self: An Exploration of the Role of the School in Promoting Self-understanding*. New York: Teachers College Press, Columbia University, 1952.
Kelley, E. C. *Education for What is Real*. New York: Harper & Row, 1947.
La Benne, W. D., and Greene, B. I. *Educational Implications of Self-concept Theory*. Pacific Palisades, Calif.: Goodyear, 1969.
Patterson, C. H. "Phenomenological Psychology." *Personnel Guidance Journal*, 43 (1965): 997–1005.
Purkey, W. W. *Self-concept and School Achievement*. Englewood Cliffs, N.J.: Prentice-Hall, 1970.
Rosenthal, R., and Jacobsen, L. *Pygmalion in the Classroom*. New York: Holt, Rinehart & Winston, 1968.
Wann, T. W., ed. *Behaviorism and Phenomenology: Contrasting Bases for Modern Psychology*. Chicago: University of Chicago Press, 1964.

Combs

Combs, A. W. "Intelligence from a Perceptual Point of View." *Journal of Abnormal and Social Psychology*, 47 (1952): 662–673.
Combs, A. W., chairman. *Perceiving, Behaving, Becoming: A New Focus for Education*. Washington, D.C.: Association for Supervision and Curriculum Development, 1962.
Combs, A. W. *The Florida Studies in the Helping Professions*. Gainesville: University of Florida Press, 1969.
Combs, A. W. *The Professional Education of Teachers: A Perceptual View of Teacher Preparation*. Boston: Allyn & Bacon, 1965.
Combs, A. W., and Snygg, D. *Individual Behavior*. rev. ed. New York: Harper & Row. 1959.
Combs, A. W., and Soper, D. W. *The Relationship of Child Perceptions to Achievement and Behavior in the Early School Years*. Cooperative Research Project No. 814. Gainesville: University of Florida Press, 1963.

Rogers

Rogers, C. R. *Client-centered Therapy*. Boston: Houghton Mifflin, 1951.
Rogers, C. R. *Freedom to Learn: A View of What Education Might Become*. Columbus, Ohio: Merrill, 1969.
Rogers, C. R., et al. *Nebraska Symposium on Motivation*, edited by M. R. Jones, 11. Lincoln: University of Nebraska Press, 1963.
Rogers, C. R. *On Becoming a Person*. Boston: Houghton Mifflin, 1961.

Freudian and neo-Freudian theory

Blum, G. S. *Psychoanalytic Theories of Personality*. New York: McGraw-Hill, 1953.
Fromm, E. *Escape from Freedom*. New York: Holt, Rinehart & Winston, 1941.

Hall, C. S. *A Primer of Freudian Psychology.* New York: New American Library, 1954.
Hall, C. S., and Lindzey, G. *Theories of Personality.* 3rd ed. New York: Wiley, 1970.
Horney, K. *Neurotic Personality of Our Time.* New York: Norton, 1937.
Munroe, R. *Schools of Psychoanalytic Thought.* New York: Dryden, 1955.
Sullivan, H. S. *The Interpersonal Theory of Psychiatry.* New York: Norton, 1953.

Personality theory

Allport, G. W. *Pattern and Growth in Personality.* New York: Holt, Rinehart & Winston, 1961.
Bischof, L. J. *Interpreting Personality Theories.* New York: Harper & Row, 1964.
Hall, C. S., and Lindzey, G. *Theories of Personality.* 3rd ed. New York: Wiley, 1970.
Lundin, R. W. *Personality: A Behavioral Approach.* New York: Macmillan, 1969.
Maddi, S. *Personality Theories: A Comparative Analysis.* Homewood, Ill.: Dorsey Press, 1968.
Sarason, I. G. *Personality: An Objective Approach.* New York: Wiley, 1966.
Sahakian, W. S. *Psychology of Personality: Readings in Theory.* Chicago: Rand McNally, 1965.
Worchel, P., and Byrne, D., eds. *Personality Change.* New York: Wiley, 1964.

Mental health theory

Barman, A. S. *Mental Health in Classrooms and Corridor.* Racine, Wis.: Western, 1968.
Bonney, M. E. *Mental Health in Education.* Boston: Allyn & Bacon, 1960.
Clarizio, H. F. *Mental Health and the Educative Process: Selected Readings.* Chicago: Rand McNally, 1969.
Coleman, J. C. *Personality Dynamics and Effective Behavior.* Chicago: Scott, Foresman, 1960.
Crow, L. D. *The Psychology of Human Adjustment.* New York: Knopf, 1967.
Grossack, M. M., ed. *Mental Health and Segregation.* New York: Springer, 1963.
Jersild, A. *When Teachers Face Themselves.* New York: Teachers College Press, Columbia University, 1968.
Kanner, L. *Child Psychiatry.* 3rd ed. Springfield, Ill.: Thomas, 1957.
Kessler, J. W. *Psychopathology of Childhood.* Englewood Cliffs, N.J.: Prentice-Hall, 1966.
Lazarus, R. S. *Patterns of Adjustment and Human Effectiveness.* New York: McGraw-Hill, 1969.
Lazarus, R. S. *Adjustment and Personality.* Englewood Cliffs, N.J.: Prentice-Hall, 1963.
National Society for the Study of Education. *Mental Health in Modern Education.* Fifty-forth Yearbook of the N.S.S.E., Part II. Chicago: University of Chicago Press, 1955.
Redl, F., and Wattenberg, W. *Mental Hygiene in Teaching.* 2nd ed. New York: Harcourt Brace Jovanovich, 1959.
Redl, F., and Wineman, D. *The Aggressive Child.* Glencoe, Ill.: Free Press, 1957.
Redl, F., and Wineman, D. *Children Who Hate: The Disorganization and Breakdown of Behavior Controls.* Glencoe, Ill.: Free Press, 1965.

Ringness, T. A. *Mental Health in the Schools.* New York: Random House, 1967.
Torrance, E. P., and Strom, R. C. *Mental Health and Achievement: Increasing Potential and Reducing School Dropout.* New York: Wiley, 1965.

Learning theory

Bandura, A. *Principles of Behavior Modification.* New York: Holt, Rinehart & Winston, 1969.
Bandura, A., and Walters, R. H. *Social Learning and Personality Development.* New York: Holt, Rinehart & Winston, 1963.
Barlow, J. A. *Stimulus and Response.* New York: Harper & Row, 1968.
Bigge, M. L. *Learning Theories for Teachers.* New York: Harper & Row, 1964.
Bugelski, B. R. *The Psychology of Learning Applied to Teaching.* New York: Bobbs-Merrill, 1964.
Ellis, H. *The Transfer of Learning.* New York: Macmillan, 1965.
Gagne, R. M. *The Conditions of Learning.* 2nd ed. New York: Holt, Rinehart & Winston, 1970.
Hilgard, E. R., et al. *Theories of Learning and Instruction.* Chicago: University of Chicago Press, 1964.
Hill, W. F. *Learning: A Survey of Psychological Interpretations.* San Francisco: Chandler, 1963.
Kibler, R. J.; Barker, L. L.; and Miles, D. T. *Behavioral Objectives and Instruction.* Boston: Allyn & Bacon, 1970.
Miller, N. E., and Dollard, J. *Social Learning and Imitation.* New Haven: Yale University Press, 1941.
Mowrer, O. H. *Learning Theory and Behavior.* New York: Wiley, 1960.
National Society for the Study of Education. *Theories of Learning and Instruction.* Sixty-third Yearbook of the N.S.S.E., Part I. Chicago: University of Chicago Press, 1964.
Newell, J. M. *Student's Guide to Gagne's The Conditions of Learning.* New York: Holt, Rinehart & Winston, 1970..
Wolpe, J., et al. *The Conditioning Therapies.* New York: Holt, Rinehart & Winston, 1964.

Skinner

Evans, R. I. *Skinner: The Man and His Ideas.* New York: Dutton, 1968.
Madsen, C. H., Jr., and Madsen, C. K. *Teaching/Discipline: Behavioral Principles Toward a Positive Approach.* Boston: Allyn & Bacon, 1970.
Meacham, M. S., and Wiesen, A. E. *Changing Classroom Behavior: A Manual for Precision Teaching.* Scranton, Pa.: International, 1969.
Neale, D. C. "A Matter of Shaping." *Phi Delta Kappan,* 47 (1966): 375–378.
Patterson, G. R., and Gullion, M. E. *Living with Children.* Champaigne, Ill.: Research Press, 1968.
Popham, D. J., and Baker, E. L. *Establishing Instructional Goals.* Englewood Cliffs, N.J.: Prentice-Hall, 1970.
Popham, D. J., and Baker, E. L. *Planning an Instructional Sequence.* Englewood Cliffs, N.J.: Prentice-Hall, 1970.
Popham, D. J., and Baker, E. L. *Systematic Instruction.* Englewood Cliffs, N.J.: Prentice-Hall, 1970.

Skinner, B. F. *Contingencies of Reinforcement.* New York: Appleton-Century-Crofts, 1969.
Skinner, B. F. *Science and Human Behavior.* New York: Macmillan, 1953.
Skinner, B. F. *The Technology of Teaching.* New York: Appleton-Century-Crofts, 1968.
Skinner, B. F. *Verbal Behavior.* New York: Appleton-Century-Crofts, 1957.

Cognitive theory

Anderson, R. C., and Ausubel, D. P. *Readings in the Psychology of Cognition.* New York: Holt, Rinehart & Winston, 1965.
Ausubel, D. P. *The Psychology of Meaningful Verbal Learning.* New York: Grune & Stratton, 1963.
Bloom, B. S., et al., eds. *Taxonomy of Educational Objectives, Handbook I: Cognitive Domain.* New York: David McKay, 1956.
Bruner, J. S. *Studies in Cognitive Growth.* New York: Wiley, 1966.
Bruner, J. S. *Toward a Theory of Instruction.* Cambridge, Mass.: Belknap Press of Harvard, 1960.
Bruner, J. S.; Goodnow, J. L.; and Austin, G. A. *A Study of Thinking.* New York: Wiley, 1956.
Harper, R. J., et al. *The Cognitive Processes: Readings.* Englewood Cliffs, N.J.: Prentice-Hall, 1964.
Hunt, J. McV. *Intelligence and Experience.* New York: Ronald Press, 1961.
Jensen, A. R., et al. *Environment, Heredity and Intelligence.* Cambridge, Mass.: Harvard Educational Review, 1969.
Meeker, M. *The Structure of the Intellect.* Columbus, Ohio: Merrill, 1969.

Piaget

Almy, M., et al. *Young Children's Thinking: Studies of Some Aspects of Piaget's Theory.* New York: Teachers College Press, Columbia University, 1966.
Beard, R. M. *An Outline of Piaget's Developmental Psychology for Students and Teachers.* New York: Basic Books, 1969.
Flavell, J. H. *The Developmental Psychology of Jean Piaget.* Princeton, N.J.: Van Nostrand, 1963.
Furth, H. G. *Piaget and Knowledge: Theoretical Foundations.* Englewood Cliffs, N.J.: Prentice-Hall, 1969.
Furth, H. G. *Piaget for Teachers.* Englewood Cliffs, N.J.: Prentice-Hall, 1970.
Ginsberg, H., and Opper, S. *Piaget's Theory of Intellectual Development: An Introduction.* Englewood Cliffs, N.J.: Prentice-Hall, 1969.
Inhelder, B., and Piaget, J. *Growth of Logical Thinking from Childhood to Adolescence: An Essay on the Construction of Formal Operational Structures.* New York: Basic Books, 1958.
Piaget, J. "The Attainment of Invariants and Reversible Operations in the Development of Thinking." *Social Research,* 30 (1963): 283–300.
Piaget, J., and Inhelder, B. *The Psychology of the Child.* New York: Basic Books, 1969.
Sullivan, E. *Piaget and the School Curriculum: A Critical Appraisal.* Bulletin No. 2. Ontario, Canada: The Ontario Institute for Studies in Education, 1967.

Developmental psychology

Almy, M. *Ways of Studying Children.* New York: Teachers College Press, Columbia University, 1969.

Ausubel, D. P. *Theory and Problems of Adolescent Development.* New York: Grune & Stratton, 1954.

Ausubel, D. P. *Theory and Problems of Child Development.* New York: Grune & Stratton, 1958.

Baldwin, A. L. *Theories of Child Development.* New York: Wiley, 1967.

Baller, W. *Readings in the Psychology of Human Growth and Development.* New York: Holt, Rinehart & Winston, 1969.

Baller, W., and Charles, D. *Psychology of Human Growth and Development.* 2nd ed. New York: Holt, Rinehart & Winston, 1968.

Bischof, L. J. *Adult Psychology.* New York: Harper & Row, 1969.

Erikson, E. H. *Childhood and Society.* 2nd ed. New York: Norton, 1963.

Evans, E. D. *Adolescents: Readings in Behavior and Development.* Hinsdale, Ill.: Dryden Press, 1970.

Frank, M., and Frank, L. K. *Your Adolescent at Home and in School.* New York: New American Library, 1959.

Gale, R. F. *Developmental Behavior: A Humanistic Approach.* London: Collier-Macmillan, 1969.

Gordon, I. J. *Human Development: From Birth Through Adolescence.* 2nd ed. New York: Harper & Row, 1969.

Havighurst, R. *Developmental Tasks and Education.* New York: Longmans, Green, 1952.

Jersild, A. T. *Child Psychology.* 6th ed. Englewood Cliffs, N.J.: Prentice-Hall, 1968.

Maier, H. W. *Three Theories of Child Development.* rev. ed. New York: Harper & Row, 1969.

McCandless, B. R. *Adolescents: Behavior and Development.* Hinsdale, Ill.: Dryden Press, 1970.

Mussen, P. H.; Congar, J. J.; and Kagan, J. *Child Development and Personality.* 3rd ed. New York: Harper & Row, 1969.

Mussen, P. H.; Congar, J. J.; and Kagan, J. *Readings in Child Development and Personality.* 2nd ed. New York: Harper & Row, 1969.

Muuss, R. E. *Theories of Adolescence.* 2nd ed. New York: Knopf, 1968.

National Society for the Study of Education. *Child Psychology.* Sixty-second Yearbook of the N.S.S.E., Part I. Chicago: University of Chicago Press, 1954.

Sears, R. R.; Maccoby, E.; and Levin, H. *Patterns of Child Rearing.* New York: Harper & Row, 1957.

Stone, L., and Church, J. *Childhood and Adolescence: A Psychology of the Growing Person.* 2nd ed. New York: Random House, 1968.

Stott, L. H. *Child Development: An Individual Longitudinal Approach.* New York: Holt, Rinehart & Winston, 1967.

Social class theory

Bereiter, C., and Engelmann, S. *Teaching Disadvantaged Preschool Children.* Englewood Cliffs, N.J.: Prentice-Hall, 1966.

Bettleheim, B., and Janowitz, M. *Social Change and Prejudice. Including Dynamics of Prejudice.* Glencoe, Ill.: Free Press, 1964.

Brofenbrenner, U. "The Changing American Child: A Speculative Analysis." *Journal of Social Issues,* 17 (1961): 6–18.

Deutsch, M., et al. *Social Class, Race, and Psychological Development.* New York: Holt, Rinehart & Winston, 1968.

Deutsch, M., et al. *The Disadvantaged Child: Studies of the Social Environment and the Learning Process.* New York: Basic Books, 1968.

Harrington, M. *The Other America: Poverty in the U.S.* New York: Macmillan, 1963.

Hunt, J. McV. *The Challenge of Incompetence and Poverty: Papers on the Role of Early Education.* Champaigne, Ill.: University of Illinois Press, 1969.

Kahl, J. A. *The American Class Structure.* New York: Holt, Rinehart & Winston, 1957.

Kvaraceus, W. C., et al. *Negro Self-Concept: Implications for School and Citizenship.* New York: McGraw-Hill, 1965.

Noar, G. *The Teacher and Integration.* Washington, D.C.: National Education Association, 1966.

Noar, G. *Teaching the Disadvantaged.* Washington, D.C.: National Education Association, 1967.

Pavenstadt, E., ed. *The Drifters: Children of Disorganized Lower-Class Families.* Boston: Little, Brown, 1967.

Pettigrew, T. F. *A Profile of the Negro American.* Princeton, N.J.: Van Nostrand, 1964.

Riessman, Frank. *The Culturally Deprived Child.* New York: Harper & Row, 1962.

Smilansky, S. *The Effects of Sociodramatic Play on Disadvantaged Preschool Children.* New York: Wiley, 1968.

Taba, H., and Elkins, D. *Teaching Strategies for the Culturally Disadvantaged.* Chicago: Rand McNally, 1966.

Warner, W. L. *Social Class in America: The Evaluation of Status.* New York: Harper & Row, 1960.

Weaver, T., and Magid, A. *Poverty: New Interdisciplinary Perspectives.* San Francisco: Chandler, 1969.

Social psychology

Abelson, R. P., ed. *Theories of Cognitive Consistency: A Source Book.* Chicago: Rand McNally, 1968.

Adorno, T. W., et al. *The Authoritarian Personality.* New York: Harper & Row, 1950.

Allport, G. W. *The Nature of Prejudice.* Garden City, N.Y.: Doubleday, 1958.

Asch, S. E. "Studies of Independence and Conformity: A Minority of One Against a Unanimous Majority." *Psychological Monograph,* 70(9) (1956).

Brehm, J. W., and Cohen, A. R. *Explorations in Cognitive Dissonance.* New York: Wiley, 1962.

Brodbest, S. "Teacher Professionalization: Its Determination and Achievement." *School and Society,* 97 (1969): 151–152.

Brown, R. *Social Psychology.* Glencoe, Ill.: Free Press, 1965.

Cartwright, D. *Studies in Social Power.* Ann Arbor: University of Michigan Press, 1959.

Cartwright, D., and Zander, A. *Group Dynamics: Research and Theory.* 3rd ed. New York: Harper & Row, 1968.

Charters, W. W., Jr., and Gage, N. L. *Readings in the Social Psychology of Education.* Boston: Allyn & Bacon, 1963.

Elam, S. M.; Lieberman, M.; and Maskow, M. H. *Readings in Collective Negotiations in Public Education.* Chicago: Rand McNally, 1967.

Elkin, F. *The Child and Society: The Process of Socialization.* New York: Random House, 1960.

Hovland, C. I., and Janis, I. L. *Personality and Persuasibility.* New Haven, Conn.: Yale University Press, 1959.

Johnson, D. *The Social Psychology of Education.* New York: Holt, Rinehart & Winston, 1970.

Kounin, J. S. *Discipline and Group Management in Classrooms.* New York: Holt, Rinehart & Winston, 1970.

Kimbrough, R. B. *Political Power and Educational Decision-making.* Chicago: Rand McNally, 1964.

Lambert, W. W., and Lambert, W. E. *Social Psychology.* Englewood Cliffs, N.J.: Prentice-Hall, 1964.

Lieberman, M. *Education as a Profession.* Englewood Cliffs, N.J.: Prentice-Hall, 1956.

Lieberman, M., and Maskow, M. H. *Collective Negotiations for Teachers: An Approach to School Administration.* Chicago: Rand McNally, 1966.

Lindgren, H. C. *Contemporary Research in Social Psychology.* New York: Wiley, 1969.

Lindzey, G., and Aronson, E., eds. *Handbook of Social Psychology.* 2nd ed. 5 vols. Reading, Mass.: Addison-Wesley, 1968.

McNeil, E. B. *Human Socialization.* Belmont, Calif.: Brooks-Cole, 1969.

Newcomb, T. M. *The Acquaintance Process.* New York: Holt, Rinehart & Winston, 1961.

National Society for the Study of Education. *Behavioral Science and Educational Administration.* Sixty-third Yearbook of the N.S.S.E., Part II. Chicago: University of Chicago Press, 1963.

National Society for the Study of Education. *Dynamics of Instructional Groups.* Fifty-ninth Yearbook of the N.S.S.E., Part II. Chicago: University of Chicago Press, 1960.

Rokeach, M. *The Open and Closed Mind.* New York: Basic Books, 1960.

Schachter, S. *The Psychology of Affiliation: Experimental Studies of the Sources of Gregariousness.* Stanford, Calif.: Stanford University Press, 1959.

Screiber, D., ed. *Profile of the School Dropout.* New York: Random House, 1967.

Suci, G. E., and Tannenbaum, P. H. *The Measurement of Meaning.* Urbana: University of Illinois Press, 1967.

Tagiuri, R., and Petrullo, L., eds. *Person Perception and Interpersonal Behavior.* Stanford, Calif.: Stanford University Press, 1958.

Measurement and evaluation

Ahmann, J. S., and Glock, M. D. *Evaluating Pupil Growth: Principles of Tests and Measurement.* 3rd ed. Boston: Allyn & Bacon, 1970.

Brown, F. G. *Principles of Educational and Psychological Testing.* Hinsdale, Ill.: Dryden Press, 1970.

Campbell, D. T., and Stanley, J. C. *Experimental and Quasi-experimental Designs for Research.* New York: Random House, 1966.

Chase, C. I., and Ludlow, H. G. *Readings in Educational and Psychological Measurement.* Boston: Houghton Mifflin, 1966.

Cronbach, L. J. *Essentials of Psychological Testing.* 3rd ed. New York: Harper & Row, 1969.

Glass, G. V., and Stanley, J. C. *Statistical Methods in Education and Psychology.* Englewood Cliffs, N.J.: Prentice-Hall, 1970.

Gordon, I. J. *Studying the Child in School.* New York: Wiley, 1966.
Green, J. A., Jr. *Teacher-made Tests.* New York: Harper & Row, 1963.
Krathwohl, D. R.; Bloom, B. S.; and Masia, B. B. *Taxonomy of Educational Objectives. Handbook II: Affective Domain.* New York: McKay, 1964.
National Society for the Study of Education. *The Impact and Improvement of School Testing Programs.* Sixty-second Yearbook of the N.S.S.E., Part II. Chicago: University of Chicago Press, 1963.
Noll, V. H. *Introduction to Educational Measurement.* Boston: Houghton Mifflin, 1957.
Sanders, N. M. *Classroom Questions: What Kinds?* New York: Harper & Row, 1966.
Sawin, E. I. *Evaluation and the Work of the Teacher.* Belmont, Calif.: Wadsworth, 1969.
Schoer, L. A. *Test Construction: A Programmed Guide.* Boston: Allyn & Bacon, 1970.
Thorndike, R. L., and Hagen, E. *Measurement and Evaluation in Psychology and Education.* 3rd ed. New York: Wiley, 1969.
Van Dalen, D. B., and Meyer, W. J. *Understanding Educational Research.* New York: McGraw-Hill, 1966.

Teacher behavior

Amidon, E., and Hough, J. B. *Interaction Analysis: Theory, Research, and Application.* Reading, Mass.: Addison-Wesley, 1967.
Amidon, E., and Hunter, E. *Improving Teaching.* New York: Holt, Rinehart & Winston, 1966.
Biddle, B. J., and Ellena, W. J. *Contemporary Research on Teacher Effectiveness.* New York: Holt, Rinehart & Winston, 1964.
Brown, B. B. *The Experimental Mind in Education.* New York: Harper & Row, 1968.
Flanders, N. A. *Analyzing Classroom Interaction.* Reading, Mass.: Addison-Wesley, 1970.
Hough, J. B., and Duncan, J. K. *Teaching: Description and Analysis.* Reading, Mass.: Addison-Wesley, 1970.
Medley, D. M., and Mitzell, H. E. "Measuring Classroom Behavior by Systematic Observation." In *Handbook of Research on Teaching,* edited by N. L. Gage. Chicago: Rand McNally, 1963.

188371

371.102
Gre

Greenwood, Gordon E., 1935–
   Problem situations in teaching /
Gordon E. Greenwood, Thomas L. Good,
Betty L. Siegel. — Lanham, MD :
University Press of America, [1983],
c1971.
   ix, 162 p. ; 23 cm.
   Reprint. Originally published: New
York : Harper & Row, 1971.
   Bibliography: p. 153–162.
   ISBN 0-8191-3089-3
   1. Teaching—Addresses, essays,
lectures. 2. Problem children—
Education—Addresses, essays, lectures.
3. Learning disabilities—Addresses,
essays, lectures. I. Good, Thomas L.,
1943–   II   . Siegel, Betty L.,
1931–   II   I. Title

X

OHirC   HIRRxc   83-5784

79 80   10 9 8 7 6